40 DAYS OF
FAITH

Wisdom for Walking
by Faith Each Day

ROGER PATTERSON

© 2025 Roger Patterson

CityRise Houston, TX

ISBN: 979-8-218-94066-9

Printed in the United States of America.

To the People of CityRise

*But we are not of those who shrink back
and are destroyed, but of those who have
faith and preserve their souls.*

Hebrews 10:39

Introduction

As I prepared to begin writing this devotional book, I began to search my files for messages and illustrations regarding faith. I simply typed in the word faith into my OneDrive search function, and a plethora of files came up in the list. As I dug into these files, I realized that in many ways, we use the word faith like the way we use the word love. We love our kids, our ice cream, and our new outfit, just as we have faith it will all work out, we have faith in Christ, or we have faith that our team will finally win the big game.

In 1987, George Michael released both the single and the album that would make him a star. It was called *Faith*. The chorus rang out, "You've got to have faith, faith, faith...Oh, you have got to have faith-a-faith-a faith." But this begs the question: In whom or what am I to have faith? Am I to have faith in faith?

When you consider the religions of the world, you think of various faiths, and even when you describe different aspects of the Protestantism, we use the word faith to seek to capture the essence of our beliefs.

As you read the gospels, repeatedly, you see Jesus challenging or affirming the faith of his audience, whether that be the disciples, the friends of the paralytic, or the woman who reached out and touched the hem of his garment. Faith is essential to life, and whether we know it or not, we exercise it daily. The Baptist core doctrines of the Southern Baptist Convention is called, *The Baptist Faith and Message.*

Beyond religious faith, we exercise some level of faith, every single day. We place faith in others – airline pilots, Uber drivers, train conductors, other drivers on the opposite side of a country road barreling toward us at 75 miles per hour.

We put faith in our representatives in our local, state, and federal governments, believing that they will represent our interests and concerns while they are in office. We put faith in the "process," believing that we will get the desired outcomes if we just keep showing up to the gym and doing the work. Further, we put faith in our doctors when we are faced with a diagnosis that rocks our world and resets our lives.

During my sabbatical in June of 2025, I was spending time with the Lord, and I came to my reading that day in the book of Hebrews. It was here that the Lord deposited the seeds of what you will read over the next 40 days. I was stirred by Hebrews 10:39 which says, "But we are not of those who shrink back and are destroyed, but of those who have faith and preserve their souls."

As I read it, I thought, "Yes! Lord, help me not shrink back, but to walk in faith." Then I wrote in my journal, "What is this faith?"

The very next verse is Hebrews 11:1. In this chapter of Scripture, we are introduced to what many writers and pastors call the "Hall of Faith." In this hall, the writer of Hebrews celebrates the saints of the Old Testament and the way that they walked this earth. These are the ones who did not shrink back. These are the ones we are to look at if we want to know what it is to walk by faith.

As I looked at each one, I saw that the Lord was giving me something to chronicle so that others might be encouraged to grow in their understanding of what it is to walk by faith. Since the idea of faith can seem so broad, nebulous, and even hard to grasp, I want to go straight to this chapter of Hebrews and take the time to dissect the lives of these saints and how they walked well before God. You see, if we don't understand faith clearly, it will be hard to walk by faith in such a way that pleases God. If we misunderstand who or what it is that we place our faith in, we will miss our way.

As you take this journey, I want you to know that this walk of faith is multi-faceted. Just as a diamond reveals great beauty from various cuts and angles, faith, too, is expressed in a variety of ways and situations.

My prayer is that these next 40 days strengthens the foundation of your walk with Jesus Christ. He is both the founder and object of our faith, and the One we seek to please.

Are you ready to dig in? Are you hopeful to grow in your understanding of what it is to walk by faith? Hebrews 11:6 says, "And without faith it is impossible to please him, for whoever would draw near to God must believe that he exists and that he rewards those who seek him." Let's draw near, dig in, and seek Him and trust that through this journey, our lives will be rewarded by our Lord.

FAITH IS...

Assurance and Conviction

"Now faith is the assurance of things hoped for, the conviction of things not seen. For by it the people of old received their commendation."

HEBREWS 11:1-2

The night before Steve began the process of stem cell transplant at M.D. Anderson Cancer Center, we discussed his road ahead. He was facing a 28-day journey where his mouth would swell with sores, his immune system would be taken to nothing, and his body would battle graft-versus-host disease.

In that conversation, Steve exuded a joy that could only be found in the Lord. He said, "Roger, I pray that during these next 28 days, I will be able to show people a joy that can only come from Jesus as I go through this fight." As we talked further, I heard him say, "And look, if the Lord doesn't heal me through this, what awaits me is so much greater. We have such an assurance of our faith, and I am so thankful to know where I will spend eternity."

When Steve spoke about his "assurance of faith," I flagged it. We don't often speak in these terms, but as Hebrews 11 opens, it invites us to possess this bold confidence that I heard in Steve that evening.

As you re-read Hebrews 11:1-2, notice two words: assurance and conviction. The word assurance comes from the root word that means to possess a title or deed – "a legal document to effect a transfer of property and to show the legal right to possess it."[1] Here, the writer of Hebrews is saying that the faith in Jesus that we possess, grants us the title to a piece of property that we don't yet currently live in.

He then adds the word, "conviction," when he says, "the conviction of things not seen." The word conviction here means convicting evidence – "evidence that makes someone fully agree, understand, and realize the truth or validity of something; especially based on argument or discussion."[2]

I love that this conviction is of things not seen – a belief in what is to come, what is on the way, or what awaits. As you read through this chapter and into Hebrews 12, you will see two key things that these saints were convinced of and upon which they based their lives. Those key things are a future heavenly city (see Hebrews 11:10), and the coming Messiah (see Hebrews 11:39-12:2).

Do you have this assurance and conviction? Do you know that you possess a title or deed to a piece of that heavenly city?

If you don't yet have this assurance, two possibilities exist:

1. **You don't yet know Jesus Christ because you haven't put your faith in him for your salvation. Putting your faith in Christ for your salvation entails:**

   - Admitting to God your sinfulness and your need for salvation to save you from God's just punishment toward sin (Romans 6:23).

   - Belief in Jesus Christ as the savior provided for us by God and whose work on the cross and resurrection from the dead have satisfied the wrath of God and opened the way to God the Father for all of humanity (Hebrews 10:12).

   - Confessing, through prayer with your mouth that Jesus is Lord, and asking him to give you everlasting life (Romans 10:9-13) as you call to him in this prayer:

     "Lord Jesus, would you come into my life today and save me, a sinner. I admit my sin and that I deserve eternal separation from God. I believe that you, Jesus, are God's Son who came to live a perfect life and die in my place. Jesus, I trust the work you did for me on the cross to satisfy God's wrath toward sin, and I believe you have been raised from the dead. I confess my need for you and call on you for my salvation. Please come into my life and save me today, I pray, in Jesus' name."

2. **The second reason you may not have this assurance and conviction is that you aren't yet built up in faith as you should be. Before we go, pray this prayer with me:**

"Lord Jesus, build my faith so that I know that I know you. Help me understand you and your ways more so that I too, possess the assurance of saving faith. I pray this in Jesus' name, amen."

Faith is not wishful thinking; it is a settled confidence in the promises of God and a deep conviction about His unseen reality. Steve's testimony reminds us that assurance in Christ gives us courage to face suffering, and conviction about the resurrection keeps our hope anchored beyond this life. Today, ask yourself: *Do I live with that kind of assurance and conviction?* If not, take a step of faith—whether by surrendering your life to Christ for the first time, or by choosing to trust Him again in the place you're most tempted to give up.

Prayer

Lord, thank You that my faith is not built on feelings or circumstances but on Your unshakable promises. Give me assurance that my eternity is secure in You and deepen my conviction that what I cannot see is more real than what I can. Strengthen me today to live with confidence, courage, and hope, trusting that You are faithful and true. In Jesus' name, Amen.

FAITH IS...

Understanding

By faith we understand that the universe was created by the word of God, so that what is seen was not made out of things that are visible.

HEBREWS 11:3

As the writer of Hebrews begins to look back at the lives of the Old Testament saints to encourage the believers of his day, he goes back to the very beginning of the Bible. Genesis 1:1 says, "In the beginning, God created the heavens and the earth." The very first sentence in the Bible is a sentence that must be received by faith.

Now, in the times in which we live, times described as modernity and post-modernity, we have many who both wrestle with and opine on the origin of the universe and the origin of life. If you do a search of theories of creation, you will find a variety of secular, philosophical, and theological views of creation.

Isn't it interesting that the first thing the writer of the book of Hebrews tells us about faith as we begin to walk the hall of faith is about God as the Creator? Isn't it also interesting that in the age of modernity, where science has been elevated as the highest truth, the various theories on the universe's existence, and the origin of life, are often accepted as true while still unproven?

The field of Cosmology that studies the origin of the universe and the field of Abiogenesis, the scientific study of the origin of life, both seek to answer fundamental questions about how the universe began and how life began from non-living matter, respectively. Many public-school textbooks and university level courses teach the Big Bang Theory of creation, and the Primordial Soup Theory of life's origin, to scientifically explain the universe and life.

Yet, as you open the Scriptures, the Bible begins with a God who creates the heavens and the earth. As you continue into the story of creation, you then see God who creates man in his own image, placing the "imago dei" into the man. The secular view and the Christian view of the creation of the world and the creation of mankind are polar opposite viewpoints – one happening by random chance and the other by very intentional design.

So, why does the Bible begin with creation? Why does the writer of Hebrews open his discourse on faith with creation? And why are biblical creation and the scientific studies of the origin of the universe and the origin of life so hotly contested in our universities and on our social media platforms today?

First, I believe it is because all views of creation and the origin of life will ultimately be faith claims – a declaration of what you trust to be true about where the universe and life come from. It takes faith to believe that a human evolved from a tadpole, just as it takes faith to believe in an intelligent designer, who is so powerful that he spoke the world into existence from nothing that was seen.

Second, your view of creation is the beginning point of your worldview – your framework from which you view the world, establish your beliefs and values, and find meaning and purpose. Your belief about creation and the worldview that flows from it, requires you to consider why you were created, what your purpose is (or isn't), how we should view others (as valuable because they were created in the image of God, or just a clump of cells that randomly came together), and how you view the purpose of government, society, family, poverty, and prosperity. In other words, your worldview helps you understand or make sense of life.

Consider Hebrews 11:3 again:

By faith we understand that the universe was created by the word of God, so that what is seen was not made out of things that are visible.

Because we confess Christ as our Savior and Creator, it brings understanding to us about life. We believe that our lives are to be lived in light of His purpose, that He has a plan for us, and that we will stand before his judgment seat. But if there is no God, each of us can make up our own rules, choose our own truth, and do whatever pleases us, because we are here by random chance and there is no real purpose to our lives.

This is why what you believe about creation is so important. The beginning point of biblical faith is belief in God as creator and sustainer of all things and that in him is life.

- The Apostles Creed begins with this sentence: "I believe in God, the Father Almighty, Maker of heaven and earth."
- The Nicene Creed begins: "We believe in one God, the Father Almighty, Maker of heaven and earth, and of all things visible and invisible."

These are faith statements and from them flows a worldview that speaks of a life of redemption, purpose, and eternity.

What do you believe about the importance of God as the creator and sustainer of all things? Further, how does your view of creation inform your understanding of the world in which we live?

At the very beginning of Scripture, God invites us to trust that He is the Creator who spoke everything into existence. Faith begins here—believing that our lives are not accidents of chance but the result of His intentional design. If you know that God created you, then you also know He created you with purpose. Today, choose to see your life, your family, and even your challenges through the lens of God's design. Let your understanding of Him as Creator reshape the way you see yourself and the world around you.

Prayer

Heavenly Father, thank You for being the Creator of heaven and earth, and for forming me with intention and purpose. Help me to trust that my life is not random, but part of Your great story. Open my eyes to see the world through the lens of Your design and give me a deeper faith that believes in what I cannot see. May my understanding of You shape the way I live today. In Jesus' name, Amen.

FAITH IS...

Sacrifice, Offering, and Worship

By faith Abel offered to God a more acceptable sacrifice than Cain, through which he was commended as righteous, God commending him by accepting his gifts. And through his faith, though he died, he still speaks.

HEBREWS 11:4

When I was a kid, I never really understood the story of Cain and Abel and why one offering was acceptable and another wasn't. Frankly, I thought it was a bit unfair. As I have grown in my understanding of the Scriptures and the importance of finances, I have better understood this story. Allow me to point out a few things as we look back at Genesis 4:3-5.

"In the course of time Cain brought to the Lord an offering of the fruit of the ground, ⁴ and Abel also brought of the firstborn of his flock and of their fat portions. And the Lord had regard for Abel and his offering, [5] but for Cain and his offering he had no regard. So Cain was very angry, and his face fell."

You probably know the rest of the story. After Cain is angry, he makes a plan to kill Abel out in the field. My assumption is that Cain didn't believe that the Lord would know where Abel was, just as Adam thought he could hide from an all-knowing God after his and Eve's sin, so Cain invited him to the field and took his life.

But here is the real question I want to wrestle with today: why was Abel's gift acceptable and Cain's was not? What made one gift a gift given in faith that pleased the Lord versus the other gift that was not accepted?

I believe it was both the order and care with which Abel brought his gift versus the order and care with which Cain brought his. Notice the language around Cain's gift. Genesis 4:3 says, "In the course of time Cain brought to the Lord an offering of the fruit of the ground."

Now, notice the language around Abel's offering. Genesis 4:4 says, "...and Abel also brought of the firstborn of his flock and of their fat portions."

What's the difference? Is it an animal sacrifice versus a fruit or grain offering? I don't think so, because in Leviticus, there are specifications for grain offerings.

The difference in their offering has to do with when they brought their gift and whether it was accompanied by faith. The phrase regarding Cain's offering, "In the course of time," means, "the point in time at which something ends."[3] Where as the "firstborn" means the animal that was born first.[4]

Here is the contrast: Cain waited until the end to bring what was leftover, while Abel brought the first as an offering, before he knew if any more would come.

The offering of Abel teaches us that God delights in our bringing the first to him because it places us in a position of dependence upon him. Abel brought, as it says in Hebrews 11:4, his offering, "by faith." And here is what is amazing – Abel's gift still speaks. Don't miss this! It says, "And through his faith, though he died, <u>he still speaks</u>," (emphasis mine).

Did you know that when you invest in the kingdom of God by giving of your first, your gift continues to have impact? As I write this, our church is nearing our 100th birthday. The fascinating thing to me about the kingdom and offering our gifts to the Lord in faith, is that those who went before us and invested to build the church, even though most of them are dead and in heaven, they still receive credit to their kingdom account even in heaven, when our ministry reaches people with the gospel today. In other words, their investment then, is still making an impact today! It's the most incredible investment one can make.

Kingdom offerings, given with proper care and order, will continue to speak long beyond the lifespan of the one who made the offering. That's an incredible aspect of making a gift in faith, that though you are dead, you still speak! "And through his faith, though he died, he still speaks."

Abel's story reminds us that faith-filled giving is never wasted. When we bring God our first and our best, we declare our trust in Him to provide what we cannot see yet. And just like Abel, our offerings can continue to speak long after we are gone—impacting lives, advancing the gospel, and leaving a legacy of faith. Today, take an honest look at your own giving. Are you offering God the leftovers, or are you bringing Him your first and best? Choose to worship Him with your whole heart and trust that your sacrifice, offered in faith, will echo into eternity.

Prayer

Father, thank You for giving everything for me through Your Son, Jesus Christ. Teach me to give not grudgingly or from what is left over, but to bring You my very best. Build in me the kind of faith that trusts Your provision and believes that what I give today will still speak for generations to come. Use my life and my offerings to glorify Your name and to advance Your kingdom. In Jesus' name, Amen.

DAY 4

FAITH IS...

That Which Pleases God

By faith Enoch was taken up so that he should not see death,
and he was not found, because God had taken him. Now
before he was taken he was commended as having pleased
God. And without faith it is impossible to please him, for
whoever would draw near to God must believe that he exists
and that he rewards those who seek him.

HEBREWS 11:5-6

When it comes to understanding that faith is central in pleasing God with our lives, the writer of Hebrews connects us to a man named Enoch. If you are reading the Old Testament, the first Enoch you will see is Adam's grandson, Cain's son, Enoch. But this is not the one that is mentioned in Hebrews 11.

The man named Enoch mentioned in Hebrews 11 was, "The great-grandfather of Noah and the seventh generation directly descended from Adam." He was, "the first character in the Bible to be assumed into God's dwelling place without having died first."[5]

We don't know a lot about this man Enoch, but what we can know, we can apply to our own lives.

Genesis 5:18-24 says this of Enoch:

When Jared had lived 162 years, he fathered Enoch. [19] *Jared lived after he fathered Enoch 800 years and had other sons and daughters.* [20] *Thus all the days of Jared were 962 years, and he died.*

When Enoch had lived 65 years, he fathered Methuselah. [22] *Enoch walked with God after he fathered Methuselah 300 years and had other sons and daughters.* [23] *Thus all the days of Enoch were 365 years.* [24] *Enoch walked with God, and he was not, for God took him.*

Genesis chapter five is a genealogy from Adam to Noah. As you read it, it almost has a formula in how the writer lays it out. In essences there is:

- Person A...they lived this long, then had this son (Person B) ... after this son, they lived 600 years. "And he died."
- Person B...they were born to Person A...they lived this long, then had this son (Person C) ... after this son, they lived 800 years. "And he died."
- Person C ... "And he died."

This continues for generations. But right in the middle of this genealogy the formula is interrupted. It is here that the writer of Genesis says, "Enoch walked with God (v. 23)." Then again, "Enoch walked with God, and he was not, for God took him (v. 24)."

The Hebrew word that is translated, "walked," means, "to use one's feet to advance; advance by steps."[6] That's pretty basic, I know. But let's not lose the simplicity of what it is to walk with God. This is how the believer advances in their life. We are to move forward with the Lord.

Notice also, that Enoch walked with God after his son Methuselah was born, and for a total of 300 years. This distinction of walking with God after the birth of his son is an interesting one. Maybe Enoch was overwhelmed by being a parent, and he decided he needed help. I'm not sure, but I love this distinction.

What is also sweet here is that we see that Enoch walked and kept walking with God for 300 years. The Septuagint, the Greek translation of the Old Testament, uses the word, "pleased" to describe Enoch's walk with God. It says, "Enoch pleased God."

Could it be that Enoch, wanting to walk with God, is what pleased God? Could it be that Enoch wanting God to help him advance along life's way, as a father, a husband, and a leader of his home, is what was so pleasing to God?

Isn't this faith – knowing that you need help to advance and knowing that God is willing to help you move forward?

Now, notice Hebrews 11:6 once more. It says, "And without faith it is impossible to please him, for whoever would draw near to God must believe that he exists and that he rewards those who seek him."

What are the elements of this faith that pleases God? Do you see them?

I see that you first, must believe that God exists, and second, he rewards those who seek him.

Enoch walked with God. Enoch pleased God, and he did this by believing God exists and by seeking him, so intentionally and consistently, that God rewarded him in an extravagant way – he didn't taste death.

How is your walk? Are you trying to advance on your own, or are you seeking God's help? He is a God who is pleased when you look for him and to him. When you do, you never know how he will reward you!

Enoch's story is simple yet powerful—he *walked with God,* and that walk pleased the Lord. He didn't perform mighty miracles, write great books, or lead armies into battle. His legacy was his daily, steady companionship with God. And that was enough for God to commend him. The same is true for us. Faith that pleases God isn't about perfection or performance; it's about believing that He is real and drawing near to Him day by day. Today, take a step closer. Spend time in prayer, open His Word, or simply acknowledge His presence in your daily routine. Remember: every step of faith you take brings joy to the heart of your Father.

Prayer

Father, thank You for reminding me that You are pleased when I walk with You in faith. Forgive me for the times I've tried to advance on my own strength or ignored Your presence in my daily life. Teach me to seek You diligently, to believe in Your goodness, and to trust that You reward those who walk with You. Help me to please You not just in great moments, but in every step I take today. In Jesus' name, Amen.

FAITH IS...

Reverent Fear that Acts to Save a Household

By faith Noah, being warned by God concerning events as yet unseen, in reverent fear constructed an ark for the saving of his household. By this he condemned the world and became an heir of the righteousness that comes by faith.

HEBREWS 11:7

There is no motivation in my life like the motivation I have for my family. It is one of my primary drivers because of my desire to provide, protect, and prepare them for launching out into the world. If you are a parent, or even hope to have kids someday, I am sure that you can understand this sentiment.

As we dig deeper into Hebrews 11, the writer points his finger at Noah, the man who built the boat and survived the global flood. It may have been a while since you studied up on Noah, so let me do a brief summation to make sure we are on the same page.

Genesis 6 opens with commentary on the way things are going and basically grades mankind with an F on the report card. It says, "The LORD saw that the wickedness of man was great in the earth, and that every intention of the thoughts of his heart was only evil. And the LORD regretted that he had made man on the earth, and it grieved him to his heart. So the LORD said, 'I will blot out man whom I have created from the face of the land, man and animals and creeping things and birds of the heavens, for I am sorry that I have made them.' But Noah found favor in the eyes of the LORD," (Genesis 6:5-8).

If you keep reading the story in Genesis, you see that Noah is instructed to build an ark and then bring every type of living creature on the earth, two by two, into the ark. He was also instructed to bring in his sons and their wives, and it was here, they all would ride out this devastating flood event that would bring judgment upon the earth for the wicked ways of the human race.

Like Noah's day, we live in a time of increasing wickedness simply because of exposure and ease of access to it. From a consumption standpoint, we can get on our phones, computers, tablets, or connected televisions and access news and world events, as well as all sorts of evil. Yes, we can see war and reports from the front lines, as well as firsthand footage on sites like X, TikTok, or YouTube, where the event is uploaded within moments of it happening. We can also access pornographic material for free, and social media companies push soft pornography onto the phones of our teens. We can bet online on sporting events. Our minds can be shaped in how to think through headlines, social media influencers, and messages pushed to our phones.

I'm not condemning the emergence of the smart phone, connected televisions, or the existence of the internet. In the same ways that they can be used for evil, they can also be used for good. But I am saying that we should understand that the barriers to wickedness have been stripped away by knowing a password or simply putting your face in front of a camera to unlock the phone.

Notice what we can learn about Noah's faith that saved his family. Genesis 6:9 states, "These are the generations of Noah. Noah was a righteous man, blameless in his generation. Noah walked with God."

I want to home in on the words righteous and blameless. The word righteous means upright, one who is a person of integrity. The word blameless means without malice. It does not mean perfect but instead tries to convey the motivation behind one's actions. You can miss the way, but the motivation behind missing the way is still good and upright. Then it says, "Noah walked with God." We saw in our time yesterday that Enoch walked with God and we learned that walking with God is simply using one's feet to take steps forward.

Noah, like Enoch, understood that to protect his family, provide for them, and prepare to launch them out into the world he witnessed around him, he needed to walk with God. He did this by caring about what God said and acting upon it in contrast to how the world around him was trying to progress.

As Noah walked with God, God spoke to him. God said to Noah, "I have determined to make an end of all flesh...Behold, I will destroy them with the earth," (Genesis 6:13). Noah walked with God, listened to his voice, and took action to protect his family from the devastation and ruin that sinful living was certain to bring.

I would argue that this is the very same thing that we must do. When we walk in faith, we seek to progress by walking with God and listening to his voice. As we do this, we will see danger ahead, because his righteous ways will be contrasted with the wickedness all around us. We will be emboldened to take stands to protect our families and seek to see our household spared the pain and devastation of sin.

As we wrap up our time together today, take a few moments to consider where you may not be seeing devastation or ruin out in front of you or your family. Might there be some areas that need reform before it's too late?

Noah's life reminds us that faith is not passive—it is reverent fear that listens to God's warning and acts to protect what matters most. He built an ark when the skies were still clear, trusting God's word about things "not yet seen." In a world that normalizes sin and celebrates rebellion, our call is the same: to walk with God, to take His warnings seriously, and to lead our families with faith-fueled courage. Today, ask yourself: *What steps of obedience is God calling me to take to protect and prepare my household?* Don't wait for the storm to hit—start building your "ark" now.

Prayer

Father, thank You for the example of Noah, who trusted Your word and acted in reverent fear to save his family. Teach me to walk with You daily, to listen carefully to Your voice, and to lead my household with courage and faith. Show me where danger lies ahead and give me wisdom to guide my family toward righteousness. May my obedience bring You glory and create a legacy of faith for those who come after me. In Jesus' name, Amen.

FAITH IS...

Conviction that Stands Against the Ways of the World

*By faith Noah, being warned by God concerning events as yet
unseen, in reverent fear constructed an ark for the saving of
his household. By this he condemned the world and became
an heir of the righteousness that comes by faith.*

HEBREWS 11:7

We are on day two of considering the faith of Noah. Today, I want to call your attention to the second part of this verse where it says, "By this he condemned the world and became an heir of the righteousness that comes by faith."

Remember, Hebrews 11:1-2 says, "Now faith is the assurance of things hoped for, the conviction of things not seen. ² For by it the people of old received their commendation." Now, notice what the writer of Hebrews says about Noah. First, it says that he was, "...warned by God concerning events as yet unseen." God spoke to Noah, but Noah had a choice to make. It's what Blackaby and King, in their classic study, *Experiencing God*, call a "crisis of belief." When God speaks to our lives, we have to decide whether or not we will:

1. **Believe what He has said.**
2. **Adjust our lives accordingly.**

Noah heard God's voice and he's in the "Hall of Faith" because he believed God and then he acted on it. This one-two punch of believing and acting is what biblical faith looks like. We hear God and we adjust our lives to his message.

When we do this, we live counter to the culture and if we do this long enough, and in Noah's case, loud enough, it speaks a message to the world that there is another way to live this life. Can you imagine building an ark and Noah's community coming by asking, "What are you doing Noah? Why are you building this big boat?" Noah did this for years, and his consistency to align his life to his message proclaimed a message to those who came in contact with him.

Does your life align with your message? Has God asked you to trust him, step out in faith, and take a stand that is unpopular? Your obedience to Christ might be the very thing that spares you the devastation others unknowingly are headed toward.

Noah's life teaches us that faith is more than agreeing with God—it is adjusting our lives to His Word, even when the world doesn't understand. His obedience was a living sermon, a quiet but powerful condemnation of the culture around him. In the same way, your faith can be a light that challenges the darkness. People may question you, misunderstand you, or even mock you. But your steady walk of obedience may be the very thing God uses to awaken others to His truth. Today, ask yourself: *Is my life aligned with my message? Am I willing to stand firm in faith, even when the world goes the other way?* Take one step of obedience today that shows your trust in God above all else.

Prayer

Lord, thank You for the example of Noah, who believed Your word and lived it out even when the world scoffed. Give me the courage to stand firm in my convictions, to live in a way that honors You, and to trust that my obedience can point others toward Your truth. Strengthen me when I am tempted to compromise and help me shine Your light faithfully in a world that desperately needs You. In Jesus' name, Amen.

DAY 7

Moving Forward Before You Have Every Answer

By faith Abraham obeyed when he was called to go out to a place that he was to receive as an inheritance. And he went out, not knowing where he was going. By faith he went to live in the land of promise, as in a foreign land, living in tents with Isaac and Jacob, heirs with him of the same promise.

HEBREWS 11:8-9

George Müller felt called by God to care for orphans in Bristol, England, despite having no money or resources. He famously never asked people for donations, he simply prayed. Over his lifetime, he cared for over 10,000 orphans and built multiple orphanages, all funded through unsolicited donations that came in answer to prayer.

Müller walked by faith daily, trusting God for food, clothing, and shelter—sometimes hour by hour.[7]

Can I tell you something that you may not like? You will never have all the answers before you are called to step out in faith. If you had every answer, it wouldn't be called faith. It would be called certainty. Remember, "…faith is the assurance of things hoped for, the conviction of things <u>not seen</u>," (Hebrews 11:1, emphasis mine).

Abraham, originally called Abram, was picked by God for a special mission. He would be the one through whom a nation would be born, a land and law given, and ultimately, the line from which the messiah would come, so that all the families of the world might be blessed.

But for God's plan for Abraham's life to take hold, Abraham had to set out. All Abraham had was the call of God to go to the land God would show him.

The word "called" in verse eight carries with it the idea of responding to a summons. When we get a summons in the mail it is to appear at the local courthouse to serve on a jury. Citizens who understand their responsibility to serve on a jury of one's peers take this summons seriously. They rearrange their lives, take off work, and report to the courthouse. They don't do this because it is fun, but because the authorities have summoned them to come, and they may face consequences if they do not appear.

But Abraham wasn't just responding to avoid consequences. Abraham responded to God's call because he was invited to receive a blessing from God. Notice the summons in Genesis 12:1-3:

Now the Lord said to Abram, "Go from your country and your kindred and your father's house to the land that I will show you. ² And I will make of you a great nation, and I will bless you and make your name great, so that you will be a blessing. ³ I will bless those who bless you, and him who dishonors you I will curse, and in you all the families of the earth shall be blessed."

God had a plan to bless a man, not just through a land that he would show him, or the offspring that he would give him, but most importantly, through his hand being upon him throughout his journey.

Sometimes, all we have to act upon is a call. It is as if we have been summoned for something more and greater. We feel a stirring, we sense a change, and we begin to shift our lives so that we can set out. But make no mistake, no matter how much research we do or how much preparation we make, we won't have every answer before we have to move forward. Abraham, by faith, "...went out, not knowing where he was going," and it was in this journey, that God met him, blessed him, grew him, and honored him.

Is God calling you to step out in faith? Maybe it's in a relationship you need to repair. Maybe it's in a change in vocation. Maybe He is calling you to full time Christian ministry as a pastor, missionary, or counselor. Maybe it's a call to give sacrificially. Most likely, if God is calling you, it feels a bit scary and uncomfortable. But don't let that stop you.

If God is summoning you, take your first or next step and keep walking. In the journey, you will find out truth about him that you didn't know otherwise and you will experience his provision, goodness, and blessings.

Like Abraham and George Müller, we are called to move even when we can't yet see the whole map. Faith means trusting God enough to take the next step, believing He will reveal the path as we walk. You may be waiting for all the answers, but God rarely gives them in advance. He gives Himself—His presence, His promises, His provision. So today, what is one step of faith God is summoning you to take? Don't wait until everything makes sense. Take the step He's asking of you and trust Him to meet you along the way.

Prayer

Father, thank You for calling me into a life of faith. I confess that I often want certainty before I move, but You are asking me to trust You. Give me the courage to obey Your summons, even when the path is unclear. Teach me to walk step by step with You, believing that You will provide what I need and bless the journey as I follow. Today, help me to move forward in faith, confident that You are leading me to a better place.
In Jesus' name, Amen.

DAY
8

FAITH IS...

Looking Forward to the Greater City

For he was looking forward to the city that has foundations, whose designer and builder is God.

HEBREWS 11:10

Do you live in light of eternity? Our faith in Jesus invites us to live, not for this age, but for the age to come. In other words, our motivation is not for what we can receive in this life, but for the life to come.

We see this invitation when Jesus encourages us to lay up treasure in heaven with our resources (Matthew 6:19-21). We see this invitation when the Apostle Paul speaks of building on the foundation that has been laid and the judgment of our lives where we receive our heavenly rewards (1 Corinthians 3:10-15). We are in awe of the Apostle John's explanation of the holy city Jerusalem that came down from heaven, in Revelation 21:9-27. Here is a portion of that passage.

> *⁹ Then came one of the seven angels who had the seven bowls full of the seven last plagues and spoke to me, saying, "Come, I will show you the Bride, the wife of the Lamb." ¹⁰ And he carried me away in the Spirit to a great, high mountain, and showed me the holy city Jerusalem coming down out of heaven from God, ¹¹ having the glory of God, its radiance like a most rare jewel, like a jasper, clear as crystal. ¹² It had a great, high wall, with twelve gates, and at the gates twelve angels, and on the gates the names of the twelve tribes of the sons of Israel were inscribed— ¹³ on the east three gates, on the north three gates, on the south three gates, and on the west three gates. ¹⁴ And the wall of the city had twelve foundations, and on them were the twelve names of the twelve apostles of the Lamb.*

I have chosen this portion to make a connection. Hebrews 11:10 speaks of the city that has foundations, whose designer and builder is God. Abraham must have understood that this city would be where he would see and then meet the fullness of his offspring.

As I write this day's reading, I am sitting under a tree at a restaurant in Pretoria, South Africa. With my Bible open and my fingers upon my laptop, one gentleman stopped to speak to me. He is an older believer who stopped to introduce himself to me, saying, "Seeing your Bible open, I just had to stop and speak to you." I introduced myself as a pastor from Houston, Texas, and we had a brief conversation before he had to leave.

Immediately after this, a gentleman a few tables away who heard our exchange, got up from his table and came to sit down at mine. He said, "I heard you were a pastor..." He works for the Brazilian embassy here. He too is a believer, and he introduced me to his little girl, Isabel.

Three men, from three countries, at the same restaurant with the same Lord. All of us blessed because of God's call upon Abraham, and Abraham's obedience. I wonder if we will all see each other one day in heaven together and recall our encounter at the Bakehouse restaurant.

Abraham saw the city with foundations. Notice in the text above, there are 12 gates with the names of his great grandsons, the 12 tribes of Israel. But then, beyond his great grandsons, there were 12 foundations with the names of the 12 Apostles. These men were the ones who carried the great commission of Jesus to go to all the nations of the world, and through their message, there would be a great ingathering of people from every nation tribe and tongue.

Abraham looked forward to that city and that day, as it says in Hebrews 11:13, "These all died in faith, not having received the things promised, but having seen them and greeted them from afar, and having acknowledged that they were strangers and exiles on the earth."

Abraham, in faith, saw what God had prepared for him and his offspring. What do you see? Do you see beyond this life into eternity? Do you see the potential you have in leading your entire family to spend eternity together and with Jesus? Do you see the people around you who need to know about this coming city and their invitation to enter it as well? Do you live in light of eternity? If you don't yet see and live this way, ask God to show you what it means for you to walk by a faith that lives in light of eternity.

Abraham's faith was anchored not in tents, land, or earthly security, but in the eternal city God Himself was building. He lived as a stranger here because his eyes were fixed on his true home. That same promise is ours in Christ. One day we will walk through those gates of pearl and stand in the presence of Jesus. Until then, we are called to live as people who know this world is not our home. Today, lift your eyes from the temporary to the eternal. Let the vision of God's greater city shape how you love, give, and lead. Ask Him to align your daily choices with the reality of your heavenly citizenship.

Prayer

Father, thank You for preparing a city with foundations that can never be shaken. Forgive me for the times I've lived as though this world were all there is. Teach me to see beyond what is temporary and to fix my eyes on what is eternal. Help me lead my family and influence others with a vision of Your heavenly kingdom, so that we might walk together in faith toward the better home You have promised. In Jesus' name, Amen.

DAY 9

FAITH IS...

Believing that Promises Made will be Kept

By faith Sarah herself received power to conceive, even when she was past the age, since she considered him faithful who had promised.

HEBREWS 11:11

How long should we wait?

That's a common question, isn't it? Whether you are at Whataburger (you know they always take longer, but it's worth it because it's fresh!), at a restaurant waiting for a table, or waiting to hear from the adoption agency for that longing fulfilled, waiting is difficult.

Waiting can range from being annoying because your burger is taking too long, to deeply painful because of the depths of your heart's cry. We aren't prone to waiting, are we?

Consider the length of the journey of Sarah and Abraham's waiting. In Genesis 12, we see the first promise of offspring. Genesis 12:7a states, "Then the Lord appeared to Abram and said, 'To your offspring I will give this land.'" In Genesis 12, we learn that Abraham was 75 years old. If you remember, it was Sarah who encouraged Abraham to go into Hagar so that he could have a son through her. She had concluded that she wouldn't be the one to give him children when she was 65 years of age.

Yet, in Genesis 17:15-17, we see these words:

"And God said to Abraham, 'As for Sarai your wife, you shall not call her name Sarai, but Sarah shall be her name. [16] I will bless her, and moreover, I will give you a son by her. I will bless her, and she shall become nations; kings of peoples shall come from her.' [17] Then Abraham fell on his face and laughed and said to himself, 'Shall a child be born to a man who is a hundred years old? Shall Sarah, who is ninety years old, bear a child?'"

24 years after Genesis 12, three angels come to Abraham and Sarah's tent. It is here that they proclaim that on their return in a year, she would soon after give birth (see Genesis 18). Sarah did conceive and gave birth. The scripture records the event this way in Genesis 21:5-7:

[5]"Abraham was a hundred years old when his son Isaac was born to him. [6] And Sarah said, 'God has made laughter for me; everyone who hears will laugh over me.' [7] And she said,

'Who would have said to Abraham that Sarah would nurse children? Yet I have borne him a son in his old age.'"

As you read this more detailed account and the summation of her faith in Hebrews 11, these two passages may seem to be at odds. But I don't believe that to be the case. Instead, as the Lord made a promise for Sarah, a 90-year-old woman, to give birth, her reaction was one where she couldn't truly fathom it. But somewhere along the way she came to the place to truly believe that God could give her a son if He chose to. Maybe she went back in time to the original promise 25 years earlier and said, "Well, it looks like it is really going to happen after all."

In all honesty, we don't really know all of what she thought. We can conclude that she moved from a bit of disbelief to belief, concluding God was faithful to fulfill his promise. This apparent journey should help us, as her movement from disbelief to belief is far more like the journey you and I take than our being 100% faith-filled at all times.

Her journey goes from skeptical to sure, not because of her circumstances, statistics, or any other data point. In other words, the circumstances of life did not give her hope. Instead, she believed in God's ability to do what He wanted to do, and if He made the promise, He would fulfill it.

You may be skeptical, frustrated, and tired of waiting. You may look at the world around you and wonder if God is really going to work all things together for your good and His glory. You may wonder if God has forgotten you and the promises He has spoken into your life so many years ago.

Sarah's story reminds us that faith is not about having it all figured out, but about trusting the One who has made the promise. She moved from laughter of doubt to laughter of joy because she came to see God as faithful, even when her circumstances made His promise seem impossible. Maybe you're in a season of waiting—frustrated, weary, or tempted to give up. Don't let your hope rest on what you see; let it rest on who God is. Today, choose to cling to His promises, reminding yourself that the God who spoke the universe into being is able to fulfill what He has spoken over your life.

Prayer

Faithful Father, thank You that every promise You make is true. Even when my circumstances seem impossible, remind me that nothing is too hard for You. Help me move from doubt to trust, from frustration to faith, and from fear to hope. Teach me to wait on You with patience, believing that in Your perfect timing, You will accomplish all that You have spoken. Strengthen my heart today to rest in Your promises. In Jesus' name, Amen.

FAITH IS...

My Blessing for Future Generations

Therefore from one man, and him as good as dead, were born descendants as many as the stars of heaven and as many as the innumerable grains of sand by the seashore.

HEBREWS 11:12

After the Korean War, many churches were destroyed, and the nation was in shambles. Yet elderly women—often widowed or raising grandchildren—began gathering at dawn to pray, weep, and cry out for revival. These *halmonis* (grandmothers) had very little materially. But they had great faith, and they believed God would restore their nation and raise up a new generation of believers.

Their early morning intercession sparked what became the South Korean revival, turning the country from war-torn desperation into one of the most mission-sending nations in the world today. South Korea now sends the second-largest number of missionaries worldwide (behind the U.S.). Further, mega-churches like Yoido Full Gospel Church (founded by David Yonggi Cho) were birthed out of this revival—fueled by faithful praying grandmothers.[8]

As time marches on, it may seem that you aren't seeing the breakthroughs you hope for. You may not feel like you are making a significant impact and that time is quickly slipping away. I am sure that Abraham and Sarah may have felt that way, yet they continued to walk with God and He blessed them. That blessing is still rippling throughout history.

Did you know that your time on this earth can influence generations? Consider Psalm 103 for a moment. Psalm 103:15-18 states:

> *As for man, his days are like grass;*
> *he flourishes like a flower of the field;*
> [16] *for the wind passes over it, and it is gone,*
> *and its place knows it no more.*
> [17] *But the steadfast love of the Lord is from everlasting to*
> *everlasting on those who fear him,*
> *and his righteousness to children's children,*
> [18] *to those who keep his covenant*
> *and remember to do his commandments.*

Verses 15 and 16 here tell us that time flies. We are here today and gone tomorrow. This seems to be a harsh reality of life. But verse 17 speaks of God's faithfulness toward what stirs our hearts the most—our children and grandchildren. This faithfulness is extended to them, as verse 18 tells us, as we walk by faith. That faithfulness to us is righteousness to our children's children.

Like these Korean grandmothers, God's faithfulness often flows through the humble and hidden. Our grandparents and elders play an irreplaceable role in generational impact by prayer, discipleship, and quiet obedience. Our Lord sees this, and his blessing for our faith is a faith that outlives us and blesses future generations.

I remember the day I realized that my children were blessed because of my parents and my wife's parents' faith. For that I will be eternally grateful. I am also challenged to extend that for my children's children, just as they have done toward me.

Abraham and Sarah's faith bore fruit long after their lifetimes, just as the prayers of Korean grandmothers still shape the global church today. That's the beauty of faith—it plants seeds that grow into harvests we may never fully see on this side of eternity. Your faith, your prayers, and your obedience are not just for you; they are a blessing meant to flow into the lives of your children, grandchildren, and even generations you will never meet. Today, pause and consider: *What kind of legacy of faith am I leaving behind?* Choose to invest in the lives of those who come after you, trusting that God's steadfast love will continue to ripple through your family and community long after you are gone.

Prayer

Father, thank You that Your steadfast love is from everlasting to everlasting, reaching even to my children's children. Help me to live with generational faith, trusting that my obedience and prayers will bless those who come after me. Strengthen me to plant seeds of righteousness today that will bear fruit for years to come. May my life, like Abraham's and like the halmonis of Korea, speak hope, faith, and blessing long after I am gone. In Jesus' name, Amen.

FAITH IS...

Forward Dreaming

These all died in faith, not having received the things prom-
ised, but having seen them and greeted them from afar...

HEBREWS 11:13A

When people hear the name Billy Graham, they think of stadiums full of people, altar calls, and millions coming to Christ. But
what most don't know is that the roots of his ministry trace back to
the quiet faith of a grandmother.

Billy's paternal grandmother, Lucinda Bell Graham, was a deeply devout Christian. She was a woman of prayer, Scripture, and steadfast faith. On her North Carolina farm, she taught her children and
grandchildren the truths of the gospel, often reading from the Bible
each night. Her influence was quiet—but powerful.

Have you ever thought about how you won't see all the things
for which you have prayed? These great saints, especially Abraham
and Sarah, only got to see a portion of what they were promised on

this side of heaven. Warren Wiersbe said, "It was faith in God's Word that made him leave his home, live as a pilgrim, and follow wherever God led."[9] In John 8:56, Jesus said of Abraham, "Your father Abraham rejoiced that he would see my day. He saw it and was glad." Abraham walked with God and God showed him that Jesus would come and through Jesus, all the nations would be blessed. At this, Jesus says, "Abraham rejoiced."

Billy Graham's grandmother didn't get to live to see the impact that her grandson would have on the world. Might the Lord have given her a glimpse of it? Might she have been stirred to pray that God would bless the world through her offspring?

Certainly, she labored in prayer and lived as a godly example. Billy once said of her, "My grandmother, whom I remember well, had a great influence on my father—and through him, on me. She was a godly woman, full of Scripture and strong convictions." [10]

Though she died before Billy became an evangelist, her influence shaped the faith culture of the Graham household. Her deep-rooted belief in the Bible and commitment to Christ were passed on to her son Frank, and ultimately to Billy himself.

She wanted a godly family with a godly future, so she was a woman who was faithful to the end. Lucinda's quiet faith may never have filled stadiums, but it helped form a home where:

- God's Word was central
- Prayer was practiced daily
- God's purposes were taken seriously

Her spiritual legacy planted seeds in her son Frank Graham—who would later host the Charlotte prayer meeting on his farm. This little-known but crucial event involved Billy's father and other local Christian leaders gathering to pray for revival in Charlotte. They specifically prayed that "out of Charlotte, the Lord would raise up someone to preach the gospel to the ends of the earth." [11]

What were the ripple effects of that prayer meeting? Billy Graham would go on to preach to over 215 million people in more than 185 countries. Millions would respond to Christ. His children and grandchildren would become ministers, evangelists, and leaders—continuing the legacy. All of it began, in part, with the unseen faith of a praying grandmother. [12]

It's a living example of 2 Timothy 1:5:

"I am reminded of your sincere faith, which first lived in your grandmother Lois and in your mother Eunice..."

Lucinda never saw the fullness of what God was doing through her life and neither did Abraham or Sarah. Yet they pressed on, faithful to the end.

Knowing that you won't get to see all that you are praying and hoping for, how does that drive you? Might you want to ask for more from God? Have you stopped to ask God to give you a glimpse of what could be in two to three generations through you and your family's legacy and impact?

Faith that pleases God is not limited to what we can see in our lifetime—it looks forward to what God will do long after we are gone. Abraham rejoiced to see the promise of Christ from afar, and Billy Graham's grandmother prayed for a future she never fully witnessed, yet her faith bore fruit in ways that shook the nations. You may never see the full impact of your prayers, your giving, or your daily obedience, but God sees it all, and He is faithful to bring the harvest. Today, dare to pray bigger prayers, dream kingdom dreams, and trust that the seeds you plant now may bless generations long after you.

Prayer

Lord, thank You for the examples of Abraham, Sarah, and faithful saints like Lucinda Graham who trusted You for things beyond their lifetime. Teach me to live with a forward-looking faith, to pray bold prayers, and to dream in light of eternity. Even when I can't see the results, help me trust that You are at work through my obedience and that Your promises will never fail. May my faith leave a legacy that points future generations to Jesus. In His name I pray, Amen.

FAITH IS...

Living as a Stanger in this World

...and having acknowledged that they were strangers and
exiles on the earth.

HEBREWS 11:13B

In August of 1993, I moved into what we lovingly referred to as the Penthouse on Chrestman Hall at Missippi College. It was my junior year in college, and I had a great roommate, Shane Scott. He is now Dr. Shane Scott, and he has gone on to practice medicine in his hometown, while also being faithful to incorporate medical missions into his calendar each year.

I enjoyed my year at MC, and I moved there for one reason only. I moved to Mississippi College to get closer to Julee King. Julee and I met two years prior at her front door when I was invited to a Bible Study that was hosted at her house that summer. There were sparks, but it took us about a year to get on the same page. In the summer of 1992, we were falling madly in love and dreading the day that she would drive her pastel adobe Ford Thunderbird east on 1-10, to 1-12, to then turn north on Interstate 55, to state highway 6 to the University of Mississippi. That year, we dated from a far, seeing each other about once every 12 weeks.

This was before cell phones, before facetime, before text messaging, and at a time when both of our parents made us pay for our long-distance bills. Let's just say that we wrote a lot of love letters to one another and kept the mail carriers busy.

The day I learned I could continue my studies for the ministry at a Baptist school in Mississippi was the day I set a move in motion. Though we would be three hours apart, her in Oxford, and me in the Jackson area, I knew that we could see each other on the weekends. She had two aunts who lived in Clinton, Mississppi where the college was, and her roommate's boyfriend's family let me stay at their place in Oxford anytime I wanted to.

As I look back on that time, I have come to the realization that I never really fit in at Mississippi College. It was and still is a great school. But I only clicked with a few people because I knew I was short term. You see, Julee would graduate at the end of that year, and we would both move back to Houston. Further, Clinton, Mississippi and Houston, Texas are very different cultures, and it wasn't the culture I was used to. I imagine that if I had gone there from my first semester in college it would have been different, but transferring in as a junior wasn't ideal.

But guess what? It was always a temporary place for me. I moved to Mississippi for one reason and one reason only – to get closer to Julee King. I was madly in love with her, and I wanted to marry her. Now, having just celebrated our 30th anniversary, I am more in love with her than I have ever been. I was willing to go sojourn and be an alien in a place I didn't belong because of who I loved and wanted to be with. And I think that's what the writer of Hebrews is telling us about these saints in the Hall of Faith. They lived different lives because of who they loved and wanted to spend time with.

That's how we need to view our time on earth. We need to make the most of the time we have been given, and we need to steward well where we are and what we have. But we are here temporarily, and this world is not our home.

As a result, we are not motivated by the culture and climate of this world. No, we are motivated by our love relationship with Jesus and the time we have here is so that we might grow closer to Jesus.

Listen to how Warren Wiersbe describes Abraham and Sarah. He states:

> Here we have the great "father of the believing" who is one of the Old Testament's, greatest examples of faith. Abraham believed God when he did not know where (vv. 8–10), when he did not know how (vv. 11–12), when he did not know when (vv. 13–16), and when he did not know why (vv. 17–19). It was faith in God's Word that made him leave his home, live as a pilgrim, and follow wherever God led. Faith gave Abraham and Sarah power to have a child when

they were "as good as dead." Abraham and his pilgrim descendants did not turn back, as the Hebrew leaders were tempted to do, but kept their eyes on God and pressed on to victory (vv. 13–16; 10:38–39).[13]

I love that Wiersbe makes it so simple. "Abraham believed God...it was faith in God's word that made him leave his home, live as a pilgrim, and follow wherever God led."

Just as I once lived in Mississippi knowing it was only a temporary stop on the way to Julee, Abraham lived as a stranger in this world, looking toward his true home with God. That perspective shaped everything about how he lived—he could endure hardship, resist compromise, and keep moving forward because his eyes were set on eternity. The same is true for us. This world is not our final home, and that truth frees us to walk by faith, guided not by culture but by love for Christ. Today, ask yourself: *Am I living as if this world is my home, or am I living as a pilgrim who longs to be with Jesus?* Take one step today that declares your true citizenship is in heaven.

Prayer

Lord, thank You that this world is not my final home and that You have prepared a better city for me. Forgive me for the times I've settled into comfort here and lost sight of eternity. Teach me to walk as a stranger and exile, with my eyes fixed on You and my heart rooted in Your Word. Help me to live in a way that shows my love for You above all else, so that my life points others toward the home You are preparing. In Jesus' name, Amen.

FAITH IS...

Motivated by Arriving at Home

For people who speak thus make it clear that they are seeking
a homeland.

HEBREWS 11:14

There is nothing like going home. Home is a place of peace, comfort, rest, and family. As I write this, I am facing about 24 hours of travel as my plane will depart later this evening from Johannesburg, South Africa for the United States. I don't travel all that much, but I can tell you that I can understand what it is to long for home. I miss my bride, my kids, my puppies, and my bed.

As the people who are receiving the letter entitled "Hebrews" are enduring suffering and persecution, the author is continually pointing them to the great examples who have gone before them in order to encourage them. Before we proceed, let's once again remember the call at the end of Hebrews 10 where he exhorts them not to shrink back. It says, "But we are not of those who shrink back and are destroyed, but of those who have faith and preserve their souls," (Hebrews 10:39).

In this encouragement and exhortation, the author of Hebrews is once again asking his audience to look forward to their inheritance in the Kingdom of Heaven. As the pressure comes and the difficulties arise, and the temptation to quit and walk away from the faith is placed before them, he is saying:

> "Don't shrink back! Look forward. Look up. Look at the saints who have gone before us and see their example. You can do it. You can keep walking with and following Jesus. He will never let you down."

Within this core message to be people of faith, he is once again inviting them to live with their future home in mind. Having pastored a lot of international students and families, there seems to always be a theme to their message when they have been in Houston awhile. That message is, "I miss home." They are thankful for their opportunities that being in the United States affords them. Yet, as you imagine, they miss their homeland.

Promise was my waitress during my visit to South Africa. She wanted to know more about what I was doing as I took a block of time that I had available to sit in her section and work on this project. I began to ask her about herself, and I asked her where she was from. That's one of my favorite questions to ask, as it communicates to someone, "I am interested in knowing about you."

Promise is from Zimbabwe. As we spoke, she spoke of the amazing beauty and the peacefulness in Zimbabwe. She then said, "But work is here, so I had to leave there to come support my family." I asked her about the work opportunities in Zimbabwe, and she said that they don't really exist and that most of the servers at this restaurant were from Zimbabwe doing the same thing she was doing.

Today, as you read this, stop and think about home. Think about the people, the sights, the sounds, the smells, and the comfort home brings to you. Thank God for home. Thank him for the people. Thank him for the rest it brings.

Now, take a moment to thank him for the eternal home He is preparing for you. Thank him for the promise of everlasting life. Thank him that you are a part of the bride of Christ and that as much as you love and appreciate your home here, you know that what awaits will be far greater.

Remember the words of our Lord in John 14:1-3:

"Let not your hearts be troubled. Believe in God; believe also in me. [2] In my Father's house are many rooms. If it were not so, would I have told you that I go to prepare a place for you? [3] And if I go and prepare a place for you, I will come again and will take you to myself, that where I am you may be also."

Deep within every heart is a homesickness for a place we have not yet fully seen. Abraham longed for a homeland built by God, and believers through the centuries have endured hardship by keeping their eyes on the promise of heaven. I know what it feels like to be away from home and to long for the comfort of those I love—and that small taste reminds me of the greater home that awaits us in Christ. Faith means living as though that eternal reality is certain, even when it feels far away. Today, let us live with our bags packed, our eyes lifted, and our hearts anchored in the promise of our Father's house. When life feels heavy, let's remind ourselves: this world is not our home, and the best is yet to come.

Prayer

Father, thank You for preparing a homeland that will never fade or fail. When I am tempted to grow comfortable in this world—or discouraged by its trials—lift my eyes to You. Teach me to live each day with eternity in view, longing more for Your presence than for anything this world can offer. Help me to lead my family and those I influence with a forward-looking faith, so that together we might joyfully enter the home You have prepared for us. In Jesus' name, Amen.

FAITH IS...

Not Turning Back

If they had been thinking of that land from which they had gone out, they would have had opportunity to return.

HEBREWS 11:15

When life becomes painful, confusing, or unfair, the temptation to go back can be overwhelming. We want to go back to what's familiar, safe, and our life that once made sense. But faith doesn't retreat. It presses forward even when the future is unclear.

Just ask Andrew Brunson, an American pastor who spent over 20 years planting churches in Turkey. He and his wife Norine loved the Turkish people and gave their lives to share the gospel there.

But in 2016, everything changed. Andrew was falsely accused of terrorism and espionage and thrown into prison. He spent two years in isolation, cut off from his family, his church, and his calling. He battled deep despair and spiritual crisis. He was broken.

When he was finally released and returned to the United States in 2018, no one would have blamed him for closing the door on Turkey forever. He had every right to return to comfort, to retreat from his calling, and to move on. But that's not what he did.

Instead, Andrew continued to speak out for the persecuted church. He expressed his enduring love for the Turkish people and his desire to see the gospel advance—even if it meant personal suffering. He refused to turn back.[14]

His story mirrors the heart of Abraham and Sarah in Hebrews 11. They, too, left their homeland. When things got hard, they could have gone back—but they didn't.

You see, they weren't just looking for a plot of land—they were longing for a better country, a heavenly one. That's the kind of faith that pleases God. A faith that keeps walking forward, even when it costs you everything.

In the book of James, we see that God uses suffering to shape us toward perseverance. James 1:2-5 in the *NIV* states:

> *Consider it pure joy, my brothers and sisters, whenever you face trials of many kinds, ³ because you know that the testing of your faith produces perseverance. ⁴ Let perseverance finish its work so that you may be mature and complete, not lacking anything.*

God longs for us to be developed in such a way as to have a persevering spirit. So, the opening line after the greeting in James' letter is to count our suffering as joy. I don't know about you, but I don't count my suffering as joy. As a matter of fact, it is the very thing that makes me want to quit. But this passage lets us know that if we continue, there is a shaping of our lives.

The Apostle Paul has a similar message in Romans 5:3-5:

Not only that, but we rejoice in our sufferings, knowing that suffering produces endurance, ⁴ and endurance produces character, and character produces hope, ⁵ and hope does not put us to shame, because God's love has been poured into our hearts through the Holy Spirit who has been given to us.

The process of choosing to thank God for the suffering, and continuing to move forward, creates an enduring spirit, shapes our character, and produces hope. This hope isn't something that is false or foolish. It does not bring shame. No, instead, it comes because in the midst of suffering, we experience the love from God the Holy Spirit. It is here, as we stay, remain, endure, and persevere that we learn things about our wonderful Lord we wouldn't learn any other way.

Friend, is there something in your life that's tempting you to "go back"? Are you clinging to the comfort of the past instead of trusting God with the future? What would it look like today to keep walking by faith?

Faith is not about taking the easy way back; it is about pressing forward into God's promises, even when the path is painful or unclear. Abraham and Sarah could have returned to their homeland. Andrew Brunson could have walked away from his calling after prison. But faith gave them endurance to keep going when retreating seemed easier. The same choice is before us. We can long for what is comfortable and familiar, or we can set our eyes on the "better country" God has promised. Today, if you are tempted to quit, don't go back. Take one step forward in obedience, trusting that your perseverance will produce character, hope, and a testimony that honors Christ.

Prayer

Father, thank You that You never shrink back from me, even when I am tempted to shrink back from You. Give me the courage to press forward when life is painful or uncertain. Shape my heart through trials, grow my perseverance, and anchor my hope in the heavenly country You have prepared. Keep me from clinging to the past and lead me step by step

into the future You have promised. In Jesus' name, Amen.

FAITH IS…

Pursuing God's Best

But as it is, they desire a better country, that is, a heavenly one.

HEBREWS 11:16A

When Truett Cathy opened his first restaurant in Hapeville, Georgia in 1946, he had no idea his name would one day become synonymous with one of the most successful fast-food chains in America.

What set him apart wasn't just the quality of his chicken, it was the quality of his convictions. Cathy made a controversial business decision early on – he would close every Chick-fil-A restaurant on Sundays. This wasn't just the start-up phase or until things were running smoothly. No, Cathy's conviction is that they would be closed every Sunday, permanently.

He believed that his employees deserved a day of rest and worship. He believed God honored Sabbath-keeping. And he believed success shouldn't come at the expense of spiritual priorities. It was a bold move in an industry where Sunday sales can account for 10–15% of weekly revenue.

Most people would say keeping stores open seven days a week is good business practice. But Cathy wasn't after what was good. He wanted what was best—what honored God.

Chick-fil-A is now one of the most profitable restaurant chains per square foot in the U.S.—outperforming most competitors despite being open one less day a week. I have had the pleasure of helping a few operators dedicate their new stores when they open. Corporate leaders come to town, and we have an opening ceremony and I would then say the prayer. In speaking to one of these in corporate leadership, he once told me that they did 10-15% more in six days than McDonalds did in seven.

But beyond the profits, Cathy's choice inspired a culture of integrity, purpose, and faithfulness that has marked generations of employees, leaders, and franchise owners. As he once said, "I'd like to be remembered as one who kept my priorities in the right order... We live in a changing world, but we need to be reminded that the important things haven't changed."[15]

The better country, the heavenly one that Hebrews 11:16 speaks of, is God's best. As we long for that kingdom and day, how can we live differently in this kingdom? Is there a way to do business differently, living by the better kingdom principles today, than just what the world offers? Do we have a chance to make a difference in how we lead our employees, our homes, and in our volunteer roles that reflects God's best? There is a better country that is coming, and there is an opportunity to choose the better way today that reflects our allegiance to the one who has granted us access to that better country.

Let's not settle for what works, but let's pursue what honors God. Let's not worry about the cost we will incur when we walk differently than the world around us, but instead, let's focus on what we will gain. Let's remember that in partnership with God, pursuing him and his best, there is great blessing.

God's best may require sacrifice. It may mean walking away from opportunities that look profitable but compromise your faith. But when we choose His way, we declare to the world where our true citizenship lies. Today, ask yourself: *Am I chasing what is easy and profitable, or am I pursuing what honors God and points me toward His eternal kingdom?*

Prayer

Father, thank You that You have prepared a better country for me, one that will never fade and never fail. Forgive me for the times I have settled for less than Your best, chasing the temporary rewards of this world. Give me the courage to live by Your kingdom values today, even when it costs me something. Help me order my priorities so that my life reflects trust in You and points others toward the eternal home You have promised. In Jesus' name, Amen.

FAITH IS...

Anticipating the Celebration

Therefore God is not ashamed to be called their God, for he has prepared for them a city.

HEBREWS 11:16B

Have you heard about the Fyre Festival of 2017? It was promoted as an ultra-luxury music and influencer beach retreat with gourmet meals, villas, and top artists. Instead, guests arrived to wet tents, cheese sandwiches, and chaos.

One attendee described it on social media: "They promised luxury villas and worldclass food... instead it was muddy tents and panic." Organizers faced lawsuits and the founder, Billy McFarland, was sentenced to six years for fraud.[16]

The greatest moments in life involve experiences that outdo our anticipation. I love talking to young couples who are preparing for marriage. In my time with them, I will often say that if we prepare well, the experience will outweigh the anticipation of it.

We have been looking at this idea of a city prepared by God for a few days now. Abraham and Sarah longed for it. We have seen that it has been prepared by God. We have seen that the names of the 12 tribes of Israel are on the gates, and the names of the 12 apostles are on the foundations.

In that passage in Revelation 21, we saw that the streets are paved in pure gold and the gates each have a pearl on them. The picture that is being painted is one of a glorious city.

But did you know that in Hebrews 12:22-24, we are told what is going to be happening in the city?

Let's look at this for a moment. It states:

But you have come to Mount Zion and to the city of the living God, the heavenly Jerusalem, and to innumerable angels in festal gathering, ²³ and to the assembly of the firstborn who are enrolled in heaven, and to God, the judge of all, and to the spirits of the righteous made perfect, ²⁴ and to Jesus, the mediator of a new covenant, and to the sprinkled blood that speaks a better word than the blood of Abel.

There is a significant word here that we must note. It's the word, "festal." It means a large (and often national) religious festival devoted to a particular deity. It refers to a joyful public assembly or festival, a grand celebration or holiday gathering. This word was often used of religious festivals or civic feasts in ancient Greek culture.[17]

In biblical context, it communicates a joyous, triumphant atmosphere—like a huge heavenly party or sacred festival filled with worship, awe, and exultation. Now, notice where this term appears. It appears in a paragraph contrasting the journey of the Hebrew people at Mount Sinai. If you recall the story, Sinai was a place of fear, trembling, and judgment. But this new city, Mount Zion, is a place of grace, celebration, and communion with God.

Here is what we need to grasp as we anticipate this heavenly city. Believers are no longer approaching God in fear and distance but are welcomed into the heavenly city, where Jesus is presents alongside a gathering of countless angels. There is a celebration taking place and it is a celebration of our salvation, our righteousness, and God's justice.

So, this "festal gathering" means that we as believers now belong to a divine, joyful, eternal community—not a place of dread, but one of worship and celebration. This is something we can anticipate and even begin to celebrate today.

The world is full of broken promises and false advertising—lavish feasts that turn out to be nothing more than empty sandwiches in a soggy tent. But God is not like that. He has prepared a city for His people, and He is not ashamed to be called our God. The "festal gathering" of heaven will far exceed every hope, every dream, and every longing we carry on this earth. We can live today with joy because we know the celebration is certain. So let's not settle for the empty promises of this world. Instead, let's let our faith lift our eyes toward the banquet that awaits us in the presence of Jesus, and let's begin rehearsing that celebration even now in how we worship, how we live, and how we hope.

Prayer

Father, thank You that You are not ashamed to be called my God. Thank You for preparing a city filled with joy, beauty, and Your presence. Guard my heart from chasing after empty promises that cannot satisfy. Teach me to anticipate the celebration of heaven with confidence and to let that joy overflow into my life today. May my worship now be a foretaste of the eternal worship I will one day share with You and all Your people. In Jesus' name, Amen.

FAITH IS...

Working by Enduring Testing

By faith Abraham, when he was tested, offered up Isaac, and
he who had received the promises was in the act of offering up
his only son...

HEBREWS 11:17

I wasn't much of a test taker, especially when doing proofs in geometry. Maybe it was the cute girls in my class, the fact that Mrs. Santire had an accent from New York, or simply because I was better at words than numbers. By God's grace, and the help of Larry Miller, I passed my math classes in high school.

Larry Miller lived across the street from us. He and Sally raised Lisa and Stephen. Larry worked for Cameron Iron Works as a blue-collar worker in their factory. He had an old 1950's era Ford Thurderbird in his front drive that needed restoration.

I remember that Larry would leave the house before sunup but always get home at 4pm each day. He was always tinkering with something in the garage, and he was always looking out for us kids in the late afternoons as we would come home and play after school.

What most people didn't know about Larry, but I quickly came to understand, is that Larry was a math genius. He was a patient teacher and truly cared that I got the concepts down. I can say that I was never his prodigy, but I survived the testing that high school math created in my life.

How do you handle testing? Do you believe that God has the right to test you? Do you agree that his testing of you actually proves your faith in Him?

Abraham walked with God. He was promised by God that through his offspring, and in particularly, the line of Isaac, that he would become a great nation and his descendants would outnumber the stars.

When God later called him to sacrifice Isaac, I'm sure his head was spinning. But Abraham endured the test. As a matter of fact, Barry Magnum states:

The near sacrifice of Isaac is recorded in Genesis 22. God blesses Abraham because he was willing to sacrifice Isaac (Genesis 22:16–18). James also identifies this event as a demonstration of Abraham's faith in God (James 2:21–24).[18]

When we endure testing, we are demonstrating our faith in Christ. James says it this way in James 2:21-24:

Was not Abraham our father justified by works when he of-
fered up his son Isaac on the altar? [22] *You see that faith was*
active along with his works, and faith was completed by his
works; [23] *and the Scripture was fulfilled that says, "Abraham*
believed God, and it was counted to him as righteousness"—
and he was called a friend of God. [24] *You see that a person is*
justified by works and not by faith alone.

True faith will express itself through works that simply prove
our faith. Look at the words of D.G. Peterson:

In a world where people dismiss faith as 'wishful thinking' or
simply identify it with the beliefs and practices of a particular re-
ligion (*e.g.* 'the Muslim faith'), it is good to have a comprehensive
picture of the faith that actually pleases God. Hebrews shows the
link between faith, hope, obedience and endurance, illustrating that
it is more than intellectual assent to certain beliefs. God-honoring
faith takes God at his word and lives expectantly and obediently in
the present, waiting for him to fulfil his promises. Such faith brings
suffering and persecution in various forms.[19]

Has your faith been tested? Have you endured that testing?
Testing isn't meant to destroy our faith—it's meant to prove it. Abraham's willingness to place Isaac on the altar revealed that he trusted
God's promises more than his own understanding. In the same way,
the tests we face become opportunities to demonstrate that our faith
is alive and active. The world calls faith "wishful thinking," but God
calls it obedience that endures under pressure. When trials come, we
can either shrink back or step forward, trusting that God is faithful

even when we don't understand. Today, let's choose to endure testing with confidence, believing that our works of obedience will show the world—and ourselves—that our faith is real.

Prayer

Father, thank You for loving me enough to test my faith. I confess that I often resist trials, yet I know they are opportunities to grow and to prove that my trust is in You. Strengthen me to endure when life feels overwhelming. Help me to obey even when I don't have every answer, and to believe that You are always faithful to Your promises. May my life, like Abraham's, show that my faith is more than words—it is trust in action. In Jesus' name, Amen.

FAITH IS...

Being Obedient

By faith Abraham, when he was tested, offered up Isaac, and
he who had received the promises was in the act of offering up
his only son, of whom it was said, "Through Isaac shall your
offspring be named."
HEBREWS 11:17-18

We are staying on these verses for another day as we seek to understand how we can live lives of faith by being obedient to God's commands. So often, our hearts want everything to make sense. We are rational beings and even the least organized amongst us wants logic, order, and understanding.

When things just don't add up, we often run in the other direction versus move forward. Are you willing to move forward with our Lord when things just don't make sense? Are you willing to be obedient first, then allow things to fall into place, or do you need them to line up just so?

The call to Abraham to sacrifice Isaac just didn't add up. Warren Wiersbe says:

> Why would God want Abraham to sacrifice his son when it was the Lord who gave him that son? All of a future nation's promises were wrapped up in Isaac. The tests of faith become more difficult as we walk with God, yet the rewards are more wonderful![20]

"The tests of faith become more difficult," as Wiersbe says, and sometimes we may never know why we have had to walk the road we are on. As much as we want the order and logic and certainty that comes with our rationale, we may just not get it. Can we be obedient anyway? Can we say, "Yes, Lord, I will obey," in spite of the cost and the potential pain?

Part of what matters in a journey with God is possessing a different perspective. Jim Elliott once said, "He is no fool who gives what he cannot keep to gain that which he cannot lose." It's a familiar story, but one that we would do good to revisit.

In 1950, Jim Elliot felt a clear calling from God to take the gospel to the *Auca* (Huaorani) tribe in the remote jungles of Ecuador—a completely unreached people group for the gospel. This wasn't a "good" option like comfortable ministry in the U.S.—it was **costly obedience**. Here are a few bullet points about Jim's journey:

- At age 22, he chose uncertainty over certainty.
- He left behind safety, a budding career, and a growing relationship with Elisabeth (who would later become his wife).

- He believed God's call was supreme—even if it meant failure or death.

In January 1956, just two years after arriving, Jim and four fellow missionaries were killed by the tribe they sought to reach. Their dream ended in bloodshed—but their story didn't.

Elisabeth Elliot, his wife, stayed and lived among the very people involved. Over time, the Auca came to faith and built a church. Jim's sacrificial obedience had opened the door for generations of gospel witness among that tribe—and beyond.[21]

In our logic, did the call make sense? No. From a human perspective, so much might go wrong. Was it costly? Yes, it cost him his life and left his wife as a widow. Did it result in fruit? Yes. It resulted in a lasting gospel movement because his wife Elisabeth also walked in obedience to Christ that on the surface just doesn't make sense.

Like Abraham with Isaac—Jim obeyed God without knowing the outcome. His obedience was "foolish" to the world, but it gained what could never be lost.

Is God calling you to a place or a people? Are you waiting for everything to make perfect sense?

Abraham's obedience in offering Isaac, and Jim Elliot's obedience in giving his very life, remind us that faith is not about waiting until everything makes sense—it's about trusting the God who always keeps His word. The tests of faith grow deeper as we walk with Him, and often the call of God will challenge our logic, our comfort, and even our security. Yet every "yes" we give to God becomes a seed for His glory and a testimony that lives on beyond us. Today, if

God is prompting you to obey in a way that feels costly or confusing, choose trust over explanation. Step forward in faith, believing that He is faithful and that nothing given to Him is ever wasted.

Prayer

Lord, thank You for the examples of Abraham and Jim Elliot, who obeyed You even when they could not see the outcome. Forgive me for the times I have waited for everything to make sense before I was willing to move. Teach me to trust Your character more than my understanding, and to obey You even when the cost feels high. Give me courage to say "yes" to Your call today, and use my obedience to bring glory to Your name and blessing to others. In Jesus' name, Amen.

FAITH IS...

Believing that God is Able

He considered that God was able even to raise him from the dead, from which, figuratively speaking, he did receive him back.

HEBREWS 11:19

As a nine-year-old boy, I experienced God's gracious healing hand. Hospitalized and in the ICU, unable to keep food down and reeling from pneumonia, I remember that my dad asked the elders of the church to come and pray over me. After that time of prayer, I sat up in my bed and asked for an ice cream sandwich. It was the first time in about ten days that I was able to hold food down and it was the turning point for my health. Ten years later, I ran into my family physician while I was waiting tables at Pappadeaux Seafood Kitchen and he said to me, "Roger, I still remember how God healed you."

Yesterday, we talked about obedience even if it didn't make sense. Today, we get a glimpse into the mind of Abraham, as the writer of Hebrews tell us that Abraham logically concluded that he could offer his son for a sacrifice because he believed that God could raise him from the dead.

Do you believe that God still does miracles? Can He still move mountains? Does He still heal? In other words, is God able?

In the Scripture, God's ability to do the miraculous is on nearly every page. It seems that only in the age of modernity and post modernity that we have lost the view of God's ability to do the miraculous.

You may be able to reason that God can do the miraculous if He wants, but because of your experience, you are skeptical that He will. You just don't see it happening, or what you do see is such a spectacle that you aren't sure what to believe.

I want to spend a minute with Jesus when he was in his hometown. At the end of Matthew 13, in verses 53-58, we see these words:

And when Jesus had finished these parables, he went away from there, ⁵⁴ and coming to his hometown he taught them in their synagogue, so that they were astonished, and said, "Where did this man get this wisdom and these mighty works? ⁵⁵ Is not this the carpenter's son? Is not his mother called Mary? And are not his brothers James and Joseph and Simon and Judas? ⁵⁶ And are not all his sisters with us? Where then did this man get all these things?" ⁵⁷ And they took offense at him. But Jesus said to them, "A prophet is not without honor except in his hometown and in his own household." [58] *And he did not do many mighty works there, because of their unbelief.*

Notice the commentary about what happened in Nazareth. It says that, "...he did not do many works there because of their unbelief."

Can it be that Jesus works in our lives according to our faith? Can it be that those of little faith see little movement from our Lord and those of big faith see big movement from our Lord? The collective faith of this town was basically non-existent because they knew him when he was young. Further, they also knew his family, and their logic just couldn't handle the carpenter's son being so profound.

What about our collective faith? When we come to worship, are we coming to simply learn lessons about our Lord, or are we coming together collectively, expecting to see our Lord move in our lives, in our homes, in our marriages, and in our church family? Do we believe together that He can use us to reach our city with the gospel? Do we have probability thinking that says, "Probably not!" Or do we have possibility thinking that asks, "What if?" Is our collective faith expectant?

Abraham was expectant. He didn't know exactly what to expect, but as he and Isaac walked to the offering site in Genesis 22, Isaac asked his father where the animal was that would be sacrificed. Abraham's response was one of expectancy. He said, "The Lord himself will provide the lamb."

Look at what Peterson says of this moment and Abraham's expectant faith in God's ability to do the miraculous. He states:

"Since God had specifically declared that his offspring would be reckoned through Isaac (Gn. 21:12), there seemed to be no hope if Isaac died. However, Abraham reasoned that God could raise the dead. He expected to return from the place of sacrifice with Isaac (Gn. 22:5) because he knew that the fulfilment of God's purposes depended on Isaac's survival. He trusted that God would resolve the problem."[22]

My friend, do you trust that God will resolve the problems you are facing? Abraham's faith reminds me that trusting God's ability is not wishful thinking—it is confidence that He will always remain true to His word, even when circumstances scream otherwise. Abraham believed God could raise Isaac from the dead, because he knew God's promise rested on Isaac's life. In the same way, I must decide if I will live with probability thinking—calculating the odds—or with possibility thinking—trusting that with God, all things are possible. The God who healed me as a nine-year-old boy is still able to move mountains, heal brokenness, and bring life where there is death. Today, I invite you to believe not only that God *can* act, but that He is willing and faithful to act for His glory and your good. Bring Him your impossible situation, and trust that He is able.

Prayer

Almighty God, I praise You because nothing is too hard for You. Forgive me for the times I have doubted Your power or limited You by my unbelief. Today I choose to place my trust in Your ability to heal, to provide, to restore, and to redeem. Teach me to live with expectant faith, believing that You can do abundantly more than all I ask or imagine. Strengthen my heart so that I walk in possibility thinking, knowing You are always faithful to Your promises. In Jesus' name, Amen.

FAITH IS...

Speaking a Blessing to the Next Generation

By faith Isaac invoked future blessings on Jacob and Esau.

HEBREWS 11:20

There is power in the tongue. James speaks of it. It's nearly on every page of the book of Proverbs, and as many of the Old Testament saints neared their death, they would bring their children near to speak a blessing over them.

As you read Hebrews 11:20, you see what seems to be a very positive spin on a fairly negative story. Isaac's sons, Esau and Jacob enter the picture. These are Abraham's grandsons. Ideally, the stories of these two would be of unity and togetherness. They were twins, and if you recall their birth story, these two were wrestling in the womb before they were born.

As the story unfolds, you understand that these two brothers are opposites. Esau does his work in the fields. He is a hunter. He is a man's man, and he is loved by his father. Isaac loved the food he provided him.

Jacob, on the other hand, is what many would refer to as a momma's boy. He was loved by his mother, Rebecca, and she worked with Jacob so that he could receive Esau's birthright and then his father's blessing that he was intending to give to Esau.

In ancient cultures, the patriarch would gather his children around him as his death came near, and he would speak a blessing of some sort to each of them. In many ways, it was prophetic. Look at how the Harper's Bible Dictionary defines this practice. It states:

> **Parental Blessing** – the blessing given by a father to his children, especially that given to his firstborn son. Normally given when the father is an old man nearing death (Gen. 27:2; 48:21; 49:1), this blessing forms part of his testamentary farewell to his children.[23]

Notice that the blessing was to the firstborn son. That's what was playing out when Jacob and his mom Rebecca snuck in while Esau was hunting, and Jacob, being true to his name, deceived his blind father.

Conceptually, once the blessing was spoken, it was irrevocable. When Esau came in from the field it became evident that Jacob had stolen his brother's blessing that his father was to give him.

So, why does the writer of Hebrews seem to make this dysfunctional moment something to celebrate? Or is there something more we are to consider so that we can understand his thinking regarding this moment?

First, we must understand that just before their births, Rebecca inquired of the Lord about these two boys wrestling in her womb. It says in Genesis 25:23:

"And the Lord said to her, 'Two nations are in your womb, and two peoples from within you shall be divided; the one shall be stronger than the other, the older shall serve the younger.'"

In this inquiry, there is a declaration from the Lord that the older twin shall serve his younger brother.

Second, we need to see that despite the folly of this family, and there was plenty of blame to go around, the Lord's purpose still prevailed. I believe that this is what the writer of Hebrews is truly celebrating.

Nate Holdridge, contemporary Bible teacher and pastor notes that Isaac initially resisted God's plan—wanting to bless Esau—but ultimately yielded when he realized God's promise favored Jacob. His trembling and eventual acceptance showed obedience when God's purposes didn't align with his own desires.[24]

Warren Wiersbe says:

"In Abraham, Isaac, Jacob, and Joseph, we have four generations of faith. These men sometimes failed, but basically, they were men of faith. They were not perfect, but they were devoted to God and trusted His Word. Isaac passed the promises and the blessings along to Jacob (Gen. 27), and Jacob shared them with his twelve sons (Gen. 48–49)."[25]

I take hope in the fact that though highly dysfunctional and of questionable character, God's ways still prevailed. Just image how much more could take place with obedient, kind, loving people!

As you consider these words, consider what God the Father did for His son, Jesus, at Jesus' baptism. Matthew 3:16-17 says,

"And when Jesus was baptized, immediately he went up from the water, and behold, the heavens were opened to him, and he saw the Spirit of God descending like a dove and coming to rest on him; [17] and behold, a voice from heaven said, 'This is my beloved Son, with whom I am well pleased.'"

What do we see the Father say as he sees the Son coming up out of the water at his baptism? He says, "That's my boy! I love him and I am very pleased with him." Those are powerful words, aren't they?

If the Heavenly Father chose to speak blessing in the Eternal Son's life, how much more should we?

As a father, I am so thankful that my children's future success isn't based on my perfection. But also, as a father, I know that there is power in the words I speak into and over their lives. Sometimes God is gracious in spite of us, but I hope I am not fighting him in what He wants to do with my children.

The story of Isaac reminds me that God's purposes are never thwarted, even in the middle of our failures, dysfunctions, or misunderstandings. Isaac struggled to embrace God's plan, yet he still spoke blessing over his sons—and in doing so, he participated in God's unfolding story. Our words carry weight. When we speak life, truth, and blessing over our children, grandchildren, and spiritual sons and daughters, we are shaping their future and aligning ourselves with God's purposes. Today, let's not underestimate the power of a blessing. Take a moment to speak words of life over someone in your family or in your circle of influence. Declare God's promises over them and remind them who they are in Christ. Your faith-filled words can echo for generations.

Prayer

Father, thank You for the example of Isaac, who—even in his weakness—spoke blessings that carried the weight of Your promises. Help me to use my words to build up, encourage, and strengthen those You've entrusted to me. Guard me from speaking in frustration or doubt, and instead fill my mouth with words of faith, hope, and love. May my children, grandchildren, and those I disciple hear from me the same kind of blessing You spoke over Jesus: that they are loved, chosen, and pleasing in Your sight. Let my words plant seeds of faith that grow for generations to come. In Jesus' name, Amen.

FAITH IS...

Blessing My Grandkids

By faith Jacob, when dying, blessed each of the sons of Joseph, bowing in worship over the head of his staff.
HEBREWS 11:21

Rev. Glenn Wagner recalls a fishing trip at the age of three, deep in Glacier National Park. His grandfather, LeRoy Rhodes (69 at the time), guided him in a quiet rowboat on a glassy alpine lake, teaching him how to:

- Sit still
- Bait his own hook
- Cast patiently
- Listen and watch for the bobber to dip

Wagner says, "Grandpa taught us how to climb into [the boat]... stay low and center... fishing is mostly about being patient, being quiet, being persistent. And mostly just being."

That dawn experience—catching his very first crappie—was more than a childhood memory. It shaped how Glenn understood his later ministry. He now views "fishing for souls" as requiring the same attributes: patience, presence, and persistence.[26]

What Glenn Wagner didn't understand, but his grandfather most likely did, was that there was a generational impact taking place in that boat that day. The lessons imparted from grandfather to grandson provided the foundation for a lifetime of ministry. The same values—wait, observe, respond—were passed from grandfather to grandson, and then from pastor to community. It's a living illustration of Proverbs 13:22: "A good person leaves an inheritance for their children's children...."

When Jacob was ill and nearing his death, Joseph received word and came to him with his two sons, Ephraim and Manesseh. Joseph's sons were young, Jacob had yet to meet them. During this moment of meeting Joseph, his dying father says to him, "And now your two sons, who were born to you in the land of Egypt before I came to you in Egypt, are mine; Ephraim and Manasseh shall be mine, as Reuben and Simeon are," (Genesis 48:5). Then, before he bestows the father's blessing on his other sons, he blesses his two grandsons as his own.

In this blessing, the younger, once again, will rule over the older. This seems to be a theme, as Isaac, not Ishmael received the blessing of God's plan through Abraham. Then Jacob, not Esau, received the blessing of God's plan through Isaac. Now, Jacob meets his grandsons and blesses the younger with the blessing of the firstborn, which is time and a half an inheritance. As Joseph requests that the blessing of the firstborn stay with the older son, the Scripture says:

> *But his father refused and said, "I know, my son, I know. He also shall become a people, and he also shall be great. Nevertheless, his younger brother shall be greater than he, and his offspring shall become a multitude of nations."* [20] *So he blessed them that day, saying,*

> *"By you Israel will pronounce blessings, saying, 'God make you as Ephraim and as Manasseh.'"*

> *Thus he put Ephraim before Manasseh.* [21] *Then Israel said to Joseph, "Behold, I am about to die, but God will be with you and will bring you again to the land of your fathers.*[27]

Then we see these words in Joshua 16:4 – *"The people of Joseph, Manasseh and Ephraim, received their inheritance."*

What inheritance are you striving to leave your grandchildren? Do you see the opportunity you have to share with them, not just possessions, but also character, values, principles, and faith?

Jacob's final act of faith was not building an altar, winning a battle, or leading a nation. It was leaning on his staff, blessing his grandsons, and reminding them that God would be with them. What a picture of legacy! Faith doesn't stop with us—it multiplies through us into the lives of our children and grandchildren. Just as Glenn Wagner's grandfather quietly passed on lessons that shaped a future pastor, so too can our words, prayers, and example mark generations to come. You may never stand on a stage before thousands, but you can sit in a boat, a living room, or around a dinner table and sow seeds of faith into the hearts of those who follow you. Today, ask yourself: *What blessing, prayer, or word of encouragement can I speak into the life of a child or grandchild? How can I intentionally invest in their spiritual inheritance?*

Prayer

Father, thank You for the example of Jacob, who blessed his grandchildren by faith, trusting in Your promises to extend beyond his lifetime. Thank You for the grandparents, parents, and mentors who have spoken life and faith into me. Help me to be intentional today with the words I speak and the example I set for the next generation. May my life point them to Jesus, and may my prayers create a spiritual inheritance that outlasts me. Strengthen me to be faithful, even in small, quiet moments, knowing that You use them for eternal impact. In Jesus' name, Amen.

DAY 22

FAITH IS...

Seeing God's Hand Over My Past

By faith Joseph, at the end of his life...

HEBREWS 11:22A

What's your fight story? During our *Fight for It* study, we talked about our various fights – for ourselves, our home, our church, and our city. We spent a significant amount of time sharing our fight stories – how God had helped us overcome various challenges and difficulties through his hand of leading.

Recounting our fight stories is fundamental to our own perspective of God's providence – understanding that God is doing something with my suffering and pain. Benjamin B. Warfield (1851–1921), renowned theologian at Princeton Seminary, married Annie Pearce Kinkead in 1876. On their honeymoon, a tragic lightning strike permanently paralyzed Annie. She required around the clock care for the next 39 years. Warfield could seldom leave her side—rarely more than two hours at a time. This was his fight story, and he was faithful to keep fighting for his home until he laid his wife to rest in 1915.

When the writer of Hebrews mentions Joseph at his death, in less than a sentence, he references Joseph's perspective of God's providence over his journey to and in Egypt. At his father's death, his brothers once again circle up without him. As they do, they fear that now that Israel is dead, they will experience retribution from Joseph. So, they come to him in Genesis 50:16-19:

> [16] So they sent a message to Joseph, saying, "Your father gave this command before he died: [17] 'Say to Joseph, "Please forgive the transgression of your brothers and their sin, because they did evil to you."' And now, please forgive the transgression of the servants of the God of your father." Joseph wept when they spoke to him. [18] His brothers also came and fell down before him and said, "Behold, we are your servants."

Once again, the vision Joseph had when he was a young man is fulfilled. Once again, Joseph grants grace and forgiveness to his brothers, while sharing a holy perspective of the bigger picture of their lives. He says in response in verses 19-21:

> But Joseph said to them, "Do not fear, for am I in the place of God? [20] As for you, you meant evil against me, but God meant it for good, to bring it about that many people should be kept alive, as they are today. [21] So do not fear; I will provide for you and your little ones." Thus he comforted them and spoke kindly to them.

What an amazing perspective! Joseph is saying, "What was meant for evil, God redefined! And he did so with a purpose – to save many people, as they are today." Joseph is reflecting over his life, and he can look back and see that God took the mess that happened to him and gave him a message that we are still learning from today.

John Piper says, "God is always weaving something wise out of the painful, perplexing threads that look like a tangle in our lives."[28] This is how God redefines the evil. Theologian Wayne Grudem defines providence as God preserving and governing every detail— yes, even the suffering we despair over. He stresses that there are no "chance" events under God's watch.[29]

Joseph's story teaches us that God is so wise, loving, gracious, and good. It shows us that God can bring beauty from ashes, hope in despair, and a holy perspective, if we will continue to trust him with our walk by showing up daily and honoring what God has placed before us to do.

In walking well even in our disappointment and despair, we are saying, "God, you are working out something bigger. Use this for your glory and my good."

This was Benjamin Warfield's perspective, leading him to a deeper understanding of Romans 8:28 and divine providence. Despite decades of suffering, Warfield wrote:

"If he governs all, then nothing but good can befall those to whom he would do good..."

Warfield believed God ordained even tragedy to bring ultimate good.[30] This too is Joseph's perspective, which is critical for the next part of Hebrews 11:22. We will this discover this principle together tomorrow, but in short, we will learn that because Joseph could see God's hand behind him, he could speak confidently about God's leading before him.

Joseph's story—and the testimony of men like Benjamin Warfield—reminds us that faith doesn't deny pain, but it sees God's hand in the middle of it. What others intend for evil, God can redefine for good. Looking back, Joseph could see that every betrayal, every prison cell, and every disappointment had positioned him to be an instrument of salvation. The same is true for us. We may not yet understand the threads God is weaving, but one day we will see the tapestry of His providence. Today, take a moment to look back at your own story. Where can you already trace God's hand? And where do you need to trust that He is still weaving something wise out of the painful threads? Choose to believe that He is at work in your past, your present, and your future.

Prayer

Father, thank You that nothing in my life is wasted in Your hands. When I look back on painful moments, help me to see Your fingerprints—even in the places that still hurt. Teach me to trust that You are weaving all things together for my good and Your glory. Strengthen my faith to believe that every disappointment can become a platform for Your grace. May my story, like Joseph's, point others to the God who brings beauty from ashes and hope from despair. In Jesus' name, Amen.

FAITH IS...

Seeing God's Hand Over My Future

By faith Joseph, at the end of his life, made mention of the exodus of the Israelites and gave directions concerning his bones.

HEBREWS 11:22

It's awfully difficult to see the future, if we can't properly understand the past. When you look ahead, what do you see? Do you see your children walking with God? Do you see opportunities to invest your resources today so that future generations can come to know Jesus? Do you have confidence that what you have invested in during this life will bring eternal rewards in the next?

As we saw yesterday, Joseph had a perspective that God had used the evil that happened in his life to preserve a people—who would become the twelve tribes of Israel. As Joseph neared his death, he looked forward, speaking about his future resting place for his bones, which meant the movement of this people out of Egypt.

Genesis 50:22-26 states:

> [22] *So Joseph remained in Egypt, he and his father's house. Joseph lived 110 years.* [23] *And Joseph saw Ephraim's children of the third generation. The children also of Machir the son of Manasseh were counted as Joseph's own.* [24] *And Joseph said to his brothers, "I am about to die, but God will visit you and bring you up out of this land to the land that he swore to Abraham, to Isaac, and to Jacob."* [25] *Then Joseph made the sons of Israel swear, saying, "God will surely visit you, and you shall carry up my bones from here."* [26] *So Joseph died, being 110 years old. They embalmed him, and he was put in a coffin in Egypt.*

Notice the forward-looking faith in verse 24, what the writer of Hebrews calls, "Joseph...made mention of the exodus." It states, "And Joseph said to his brothers, 'I am about to die, but God will visit you and bring you up out of this land to the land that he swore to Abraham, to Isaac, and to Jacob.'"

Joseph makes two key statements here. They are, "God will visit you..." and "God will bring you..."

First, do you believe that you can meet with God? As a reminder, Hebrews 11:6 states, "And without faith it is impossible to please him, for whoever would draw near to God must believe that he exists and that he rewards those who seek him." God rewards those who seek him.

James 4:8a states, "Draw near to God, and he will draw near to you..." The Bible reveals a God who visits with us as we seek Him and draw near to Him.

Second, do you believe that God can bring you and yours into his purposes for your lives? Philippians 1:6 states, "And I am sure of this, that he who began a good work in you will bring it to completion at the day of Jesus Christ."

Joseph's fundamental belief was that God visits, and God brings! This should be our belief as well.

You see, Joseph knew that God was up to something more in this grand narrative. He was familiar with the covenant to Abraham, Isaac, and Jacob. He was well aware that Egypt was never the final destination, but that the time in Egypt was used for a season to preserve and then build up a people so that there could be a mighty nation.

Joseph knew of the land because he had grown up there, and He was confident that God would fulfill His promises to his great grandfather, his grandfather, his father, and his offspring. He could see the hand of God behind him and before him.

What about you? Maybe you have lost sight of what God is up to? Maybe you find yourself in a location or season for which you didn't sign up. Maybe there is suffering, and hardship, and it is difficult for you to make sense of it. Maybe you have suffered such loss that nothing can console you.

My friend, look up! God will visit you as you seek Him. Psalm 34:5 states, "Those who look to him are radiant, and their faces shall never be ashamed."

My friend, look up! God will bring you into a promised land where there is no more crying or tears or pain. Revelation 21:1-4 says:

> *Then I saw a new heaven and a new earth, for the first heaven and the first earth had passed away, and the sea was no more. ² And I saw the holy city, new Jerusalem, coming down out of heaven from God, prepared as a bride adorned for her husband. ³ And I heard a loud voice from the throne saying, "Behold, the dwelling place of God is with man. He will dwell with them, and they will be his people, and God himself will be with them as their God. ⁴ He will wipe away every tear from their eyes, and death shall be no more, neither shall there be mourning, nor crying, nor pain anymore, for the former things have passed away."*

Joseph's final words were soaked in faith. He could look back over his past and see God's hand, but he also looked forward with confidence, declaring, "God will visit you... and God will bring you." That's what faith does—it clings to the promises of God, not only for today but for tomorrow and for generations yet to come. Even in Egypt, far from the land God had promised, Joseph believed the story wasn't over. And neither is yours. Whatever season you are in—whether waiting, hurting, or wondering—God is still writing your story. Today, take a step of faith by naming one area of your future where you will declare, "God will visit me, and God will bring me." Trust Him to finish the good work He has started in your life.

Prayer

Lord, I praise You because You are the God who visits and the God who brings. Thank You that my future is in Your hands, and that no season of my life is wasted in Your plan. When I am tempted to doubt or fear, remind me of Joseph's faith and help me to say with confidence, "God will visit me, and God will bring me." Strengthen me to trust that You will carry me and my family into every promise You have made. Keep my eyes on the future You have prepared, and may my faith today point others to the hope of Your eternal kingdom. In Jesus' name, Amen.

FAITH IS...

Taking a Just Stand

By faith Moses, when he was born, was hidden for three months by his parents, because they saw that the child was beautiful, and they were not afraid of the king's edict.

HEBREWS 11:23

Throughout history, Christian people have been marked by seeking justice. One of the ways the Roman Empire was won to the Christian faith is how Christians demonstrated just, quiet living before their neighbors.

This quiet living made Christian people stand out radically in Roman society. They cared for the poor and sick, even during plagues, rescued abandoned babies left to die (a legal but brutal Roman practice). Further, followers of Jesus rejected violence and sexual exploitation, which were common and even celebrated in Roman culture. Christians also called slaves and masters brothers in Christ (Philemon 16). Look at this note about Christians from the second century, in *Letter to Diognetus*:

"They love all men and are persecuted by all... They repay curses with blessings."

In a society built on power, hierarchy, and domination, Christian communities shocked Rome by giving dignity to women, slaves, and the poor. Many were given leadership roles. Through the ethic of Christ, enemies were forgiven, offenders restored, and justice was redefined as humility, mercy, and reconciliation.

The call of Christ is a call to loyalty to him over loyalty to governing authorities. From this, Dr. Martin Luther King, Jr. would take his stand of non-violent protest. King argued and modeled an obligation to disobey unjust laws which are not in harmony with moral law. Dietrich Bonhoeffer did the same in his protest of Nazi Germany and their unjust slaughter of the Jews.

In Acts 4:19-22, when Peter and John stand up to the council telling them to no longer preach Jesus, we see these words:

But Peter and John answered them, "Whether it is right in the sight of God to listen to you rather than to God, you must judge, [20] for we cannot but speak of what we have seen and heard."

As the writer of Hebrews introduces us to Moses, he notes the bold, quiet faith of his parents. I would imagine, like any parent, they were devastated when they learned of the call to put all infant boys into the Nile River, that they might die. But unwilling to do such an immoral act to their son, they instead, devised a plan.

If you recall the story, Moses' mother built a basket of reeds in which to place the baby. The child was placed in the basket, and the basket was placed in the water, strategically located in the exact place where Pharoah's daughter would go and bathe. At seeing the child, Pharoah's daughter was moved, and she chose to take baby Moses into her own household.

In an anticipated move, Moses' sister, Miriam, was right there on the scene and quickly suggested that a Hebrew nurse be able to take care of and nurse the child until he was weaned. This Hebrew nurse was Moses' mother.

In giving Moses up, God gave Moses back to his mother, if but for a time. They took this stand because they feared God more than they feared the king. It was this courageous act of civil disobedience that would ultimately prepare Moses to stand before Pharoah to demand that he let the Hebrew people go.

Are there people in your life that need you to take a stand for them? Micah 6:8 states:

> *He has told you, O man, what is good;*
> *and what does the Lord require of you*
> *but to do justice, and to love kindness,*
> *and to walk humbly with your God?*

Prayer

Righteous Father, thank You for the example of those who have taken bold and faithful stands for justice throughout history. Thank You for the courage of Moses' parents, who feared You more than Pharaoh. Lord, give me that same courage today. Open my eyes to those around me who need someone to speak up for them. Teach me to value Your approval above the world's applause, and to live with quiet conviction that points others to Your justice and mercy. May my life be a testimony that You are my God, and I trust You fully. In Jesus' name, Amen.

FAITH IS...

Living a Set Apart Life to Please God

By faith Moses, when he was grown up, refused to be called the son of Pharaoh's daughter, choosing rather to be mistreated with the people of God than to enjoy the fleeting pleasures of sin.

HEBREWS 11:24-25

Have you ever had to take a stand for your faith because of the principle of the matter? One of our deacons, in a new job, and at the bottom of the organization chart, was on a trip with some of the leadership. It was time for lunch, and the leader chose a restaurant called Twin Peaks. It is an establishment catering to men by employing women who are young and willing to wear extremely small and tight outfits. One might say that the food is not the real draw.

The team agreed with their leader that Twin Peaks would be an amazing lunch. This young man, with no influence or ability to drive himself elsewhere had to simply ride along. But this young man also had a decision to make when it came time to exit the vehicle and enter the restaurant.

His father, recounting the story to a few of us, was beaming with pride when he said, "And do you know what he did? He got out of the vehicle and just told the guys that he would wait outside because he didn't feel comfortable going into the restaurant."

That's what conviction looks like. It stands alone, flees immorality, speaks against injustice, even when it is costly. This young man loved Jesus more than the approval of men and so, the choice was pretty simple for him.

What does strong conviction have to do with faith? How are the two related?

Strong conviction has its roots in faith – that if I honor God, God will honor me. Strong conviction comes because our identity of being in Christ is our predominant influence. It's our faith in Jesus that informs how we carry ourselves, what we will eat or drink, with whom we will associate, and whether or not we will stand for what is right or look the other way.

The strength of our convictions comes from understanding our identity. That's Moses' story. Once grown, he chose to stand with his fellow Hebrews. We see this stand play out in his reaction to injustice. Notice Exodus 2:11-12:

> [11] *One day, when Moses had grown up, he went out to his people and looked on their burdens, and he saw an Egyptian beating a Hebrew, one of his people.* [12] *He looked this way and*

that, and seeing no one, he struck down the Egyptian and hid him in the sand.

Notice that verse 11 says, "...he went out to his people and looked on their burdens." Moses didn't have the burdens that they had. He grew up in the palace. Seeing an Egyptian beating a Hebrew slave, he took matters into his own hands.

The next day, Moses sees two Hebrews in a quarrel. Notice Exodus 2:13-14:

> [13] *When he went out the next day, behold, two Hebrews were struggling together. And he said to the man in the wrong, "Why do you strike your companion?"* [14] *He answered, "Who made you a prince and a judge over us? Do you mean to kill me as you killed the Egyptian?"*

Nearly every time I have read this, I have seen the fact that Moses' killing of the Egyptian goes public. Somebody saw what he did! But if you back up and see the back and forth between Moses and the Hebrew man who was in the wrong, you see an interesting exchange. Moses is trying to see that his people live in peace. I'm sure that his clothes were very different from those of the Hebrew slaves. But the question that is posed is fascinating. It says, "Who made you a prince and a judge over us?"

Moses could have replied, "My adoptive mom, Pharoah's daughter. I'm the son of a princess." What's also fascinating to think about is the fact that in the third phase of Moses' life, he will be the leader and judge over Israel.

But Moses' identity was never wrapped up in his address, his possessions, what he had been spared by growing up in the king's palace, and the trappings that come along with wealth. No, even here in this moment, Moses is burdened for his people. That's what led him to kill the Egyptian, and it is what will lead him to flea Pharoah's court and live in exile.

Moses convictions were for God's people and their well-being versus his own. As a result, he risked what he enjoyed in order to stand for what he saw to be right and just.

Are you willing to risk your reputation, your position, or your status amongst friends because of your love for Jesus? Are you more comfortable around their sin, or standing alone? Faith is living a set apart life that is pleasing to God.

Moses could have enjoyed a lifetime of luxury in Pharaoh's palace, but by faith, he chose instead to identify with God's people—even when it meant suffering and loss. In the same way, that deacon chose to quietly take a stand, refusing to compromise his convictions for the sake of fitting in. Faith that pleases God is faith that sets us apart. It shapes how we live, where we go, what we watch, and the company we keep. It may cost us popularity, opportunities, or comfort, but it anchors us in something far greater: our identity as children of God. Today, ask yourself: *Where is God calling me to live set apart? Is there a place in my life where I've been compromising instead of standing?* Choose to honor Him above all else, and trust that His reward is better than the fleeting approval of this world.

Prayer

Holy God, thank You for calling me out of darkness and setting me apart as Your child. Forgive me for the times I've sought comfort, approval, or acceptance more than I've sought to please You. Give me the courage to stand for what is right, even when it is unpopular or costly. Root my convictions deeply in my identity in Christ and let my life reflect the beauty of holiness. May my choices, my words, and my actions point others to You and bring glory to Your name. In Jesus' name, Amen.

FAITH IS...

Knowing and Pursuing True Success

He considered the reproach of Christ greater wealth than the
treasures of Egypt, for he was looking to the reward.

HEBREWS 11:26

I remember as a kid, that my mom once received a Christmas bonus that was different. It was special, bigger, beyond what was normal. My mom was a legal secretary at a large law firm in downtown Houston. She had been working long hours that year and would often have to stay at work until nine or ten o'clock at night.

When the bonus came, Christmas was special, bigger, and beyond what was normal. I remember one of us asked her about it and she said it came from the Howard Hughes estate. I had heard of

Howard Hughes but didn't know a lot about him. I only knew that Hughes was a wealthy recluse who died a miserable death.

Howard Hughes (1905–1976) was one of the wealthiest and most famous men of the 20th century. He was a business magnate, inheriting a fortune from his father's oil tool company. He was an aviation pioneer, setting multiple flying records and building advanced aircraft.

Hughes produced and directed films, many that were controversial and high grossing. He was a real estate tycoon, buying huge amounts of land and casinos in Las Vegas.

He lived a life of extravagance, celebrity, and innovation—often in the headlines, hobnobbing with movie stars, and reshaping industries. At one point, he owned parts of TWA Airlines, RKO Pictures, and numerous hotels and casinos.

This sounds amazing, doesn't it? Despite his wealth and fame, Hughes' life unraveled in extraordinary ways:

- **Mental Health Decline:** He developed severe obsessive-compulsive disorder (OCD), germophobia, and increasing paranoia.
- **Addiction:** Hughes became addicted to painkillers and drugs after a plane crash.
- **Isolation:** For the last decades of his life, he lived in dark hotel rooms, avoided daylight, and interacted with others only through notes or phone calls—even with his closest aides.
- **Personal Hygiene:** He let his hair and nails grow long, refused to bathe, and lived in unsanitary conditions—despite

access to unlimited luxury.

- **Death:** He died in 1976 at the age of 70. Autopsy reports showed he was emaciated, suffering from malnutrition and kidney failure. He weighed just 90 pounds at death.

Hughes had everything the world celebrates—money, fame, power, women, adventure—but ended his life lonely, broken, and tormented. He is a stark reminder of Jesus' words in Mark 8:36 which say, "*For what does it profit a man to gain the whole world and forfeit his soul?*"

As the writer of Hebrews shows us the faith-driven movement of Moses, he makes a statement that is significant. Notice again our verse today. It says, "He considered the reproach of Christ greater wealth than the treasures of Egypt, for he was looking to the reward."

The treasures of Egypt had to be incredible. They are the things that museums put on display. As a son of the princess, Moses had all that he could ever want or need. His inheritance would have been far greater than that of Howard Hughes.

But Moses "considered." This word means to evaluate and reckon. The word "reproach" means insult or disparagement. In other words, Moses looked across the landscape of his life as a prince in Egypt and saw the suffering of his family and people and concluded that it would be better to be no one with nothing, tending sheep, than to live in luxury while his people were oppressed.

Moses saw the temporary nature of Egypt and the eternal nature of walking in relationship with the God of Abraham, Isaac, and Jacob and he concluded that this was the greater reward.

As we come to our time of conclusion today, let me point you to 1 Corinthians 3:10-15.

According to the grace of God given to me, like a skilled master builder I laid a foundation, and someone else is building upon it. Let each one take care how he builds upon it. [11] *For no one can lay a foundation other than that which is laid, which is Jesus Christ.* [12] *Now if anyone builds on the foundation with gold, silver, precious stones, wood, hay, straw—* [13] *each one's work will become manifest, for the Day will disclose it, because it will be revealed by fire, and the fire will test what sort of work each one has done.* [14] *If the work that anyone has built on the foundation survives, he will receive a reward.* [15] *If anyone's work is burned up, he will suffer loss, though he himself will be saved, but only as through fire.*

This portion speaks to how we build upon the foundation of Christ in our life. It speaks to the materials that we use in building our lives, the judgement seat of Christ and the fire that will test the work we have done. Notice now verse 14. It says, "If the work that anyone has built on the foundation survives, he will receive a reward." Moses evaluated and reckoned that this reward would be far greater than the earthly pleasures of Egypt and he went for it. He didn't pursue that which was empty. No, he pursued the One who would bestow on him honor and reward that would never perish, spoil, or fade, for he knew that this was true success.

Will we chase the world's definition of success, or will we pursue God's best—building on the foundation of Jesus with what will last forever? Today, take a moment to evaluate your own pursuits. What are you building your life upon—wood, hay, and stubble, or gold, silver, and precious stones? Choose to live for the reward that only God can give, for that is true success.

Prayer

Father, thank You for reminding me today that true success is not measured by wealth, fame, or possessions, but by faithfulness to You. Forgive me for the times I have been tempted to pursue what is temporary rather than what is eternal. Teach me to evaluate my life with wisdom, as Moses did, and to consider the reward of walking with Christ greater than all the treasures this world can offer. Strengthen me to live with eternity in mind, building my life on the solid foundation of Jesus. May everything I do bring You glory and stand the test of fire on the Day of Christ. In His name I pray, Amen.

FAITH IS...

Looking to the Higher Authority for Next Steps

By faith he left Egypt, not being afraid of the anger of the king, for he endured as seeing him who is invisible.

HEBREWS 11:27

Harriet Tubman was born into slavery in Maryland in the early 1820s. She knew the whip of her master, the weight of chains, and the constant fear that hovered over the plantation. But Harriet feared God more than she feared any earthly master. That fear of God became the fuel of her faith.

One night in 1849, guided by little more than starlight and the whispers of the Underground Railroad, Harriet took her first steps toward freedom.[31] Escaping slavery wasn't just illegal, it was considered rebellion against the laws of the land. Federal marshals were empowered to hunt down and punish those who fled, and those who helped them.

But Harriet didn't just escape for herself. She returned—not once, not twice, but nearly 13 times—to lead over 70 enslaved men, women, and children to freedom.[32] She did it without weapons, wealth, or political power. Instead, she carried a Bible, a fierce trust in God,[33] and a quiet resolve that whispered, *"I will not bow to Pharaoh, because I bow to the Lord."*

She famously said:

"I never ran my train off the track, and I never lost a passenger."[34]

Harriet's courage didn't come from the absence of fear—it came from a greater fear. She feared disobeying God more than she feared man. Because of that, she changed the course of history. The line "I will not bow to Pharaoh, because I bow to the Lord" is a thematic summary that draws on Exodus-like imagery that Tubman often referenced herself, seeing her mission in terms of Moses leading the people out of Egypt.

Standing for what's right in the face of an authority takes great courage. The writer of Hebrews is helping us understand the faith of Moses, and his summation of Moses' actions to flee Egypt are noted as steps of faith because of his view of God. As you read the story in Exodus 2, you see that Moses flees Egypt because Pharoah is looking to kill him.

To this point in Exodus 2, we see that Moses is burdened for the Hebrew people. He knows it is not right that they are enslaved. He sees the injustice of their suffering, and his actions are to help remedy this injustice, despite the law of the land.

There are other biblical examples of taking a stand against the law of the land because of one's faith. Daniel doesn't stop praying to God because there is a new law passed. David, the young giant slayer, shepherd, poet, and musician, fled the service of King Saul, having tried to work within the system and serve the king. But he was unable to, as King Saul hurled a spear at David, trying to end his life. Daniel stayed within the system to influence it, while David took himself out of the situation and went into the desert lands of Israel.

Both Moses and David spent time wandering—Moses in Midian, and David in the Negev. Both men took next steps in their life to build a family and establish themselves. Then, both men responded to God's next step for their lives to lead, influence, and grow a nation. But neither of them could do it inside the system in which they were placed. To do so, for Moses would have been immoral, as Pharoah was not going to alleviate the burdens of the Hebrew people. To stay within the system for David would be deadly, as the king's jealousy sought to destroy him.

There are times that to do the right thing that honors God, we work within the system to influence and lead change. William Wilberforce's 45 years in British Parliament shows us this – one who yearly would introduce legislation for the abolishment of the slave trade in the British Empire.

Then there are times that we must step outside of the system to take the next step for the justice we seek. Moses, Daniel, David,

Harriet Tubman, and William Wilberforce, all remind us that true faith doesn't bow to earthly powers when they conflict with God's will. Each of them recognized a higher authority, the One who is invisible yet ever present and sovereign. Faith gave them the courage to either work within broken systems or to step outside of them when obedience to God demanded it. Their example challenges us to ask: *Where am I tempted to bow to the pressures of people, culture, or authority instead of bowing to the Lord?* Today, take a step of faith by choosing God's voice over every competing voice. Ask Him to show you clearly where He is calling you to stand, speak, or step forward in obedience.

Prayer

Father, thank You for reminding me that You are the higher authority, the One who sees all and rules over all. Give me the courage to fear You more than I fear people, laws, or circumstances. Like Moses, Daniel, David, and Harriet Tubman, help me to listen for Your voice and walk faithfully, even when it means standing against the flow of culture or taking a path that feels uncertain. Strengthen my heart to endure as one who sees You—the invisible yet ever-present God. Today, I choose to bow before You alone. In Jesus' name, Amen.

FAITH IS...

Applying the Blood of the Lamb

By faith he kept the Passover and sprinkled the blood, so that the Destroyer of the firstborn might not touch them.

HEBREWS 10:28

In one sentence, the writer of Hebrews has just moved the reader through 40 years of the story, bypassing Moses' time in Midian, the theophany of the burning bush, and the first nine plagues.

Before Moses instructs the people about the tenth plague, the death of the firstborn, he appears before Pharoah and warns him of the utter heartache and devastation that is coming. Exodus 11:2-6 states:

So Moses said, "Thus says the Lord: 'About midnight I will go out in the midst of Egypt, ⁵ and every firstborn in the land of Egypt shall die, from the firstborn of Pharaoh who sits on his

throne, even to the firstborn of the slave girl who is behind the
handmill, and all the firstborn of the cattle. ⁶ *There shall be a*
great cry throughout all the land of Egypt, such as there has
never been, nor ever will be again."

Moses has just issued a preemptive warning that judgment is
coming. He tells Pharoah that his firstborn will be killed, along with
everyone else's firstborn. He even proclaims that the firstborn of the
cattle will die. Egypt has never seen the judgment or devastation like
they are about to encounter.

Now, here is my question: If you were Pharoah, and you have
seen the nine previous plagues, and you are warned that your son is
going to be killed in this plague, aren't you willing to let up, and let
the Hebrew people go? Since Moses and Aaron have arrived, there
has been nothing but severe trouble. But Exodus 11:10 lets us know
that Pharoah isn't budging.

As Exodus 12 opens, Moses and Aaron tell the people the game
plan. Essentially, on the 10th day of the month, select a lamb that
is unblemished. On the 14th at twilight, everyone is to go out and
slaughter the lamb.

With the blood of the lamb, take it and paint the doorposts.
Then, with the body of the animal, they were to roast it and then eat
it in haste. It says in Exodus 12:11-13:

In this manner you shall eat it: with your belt fastened, your
sandals on your feet, and your staff in your hand. And you
shall eat it in haste. It is the Lord's Passover. ¹² *For I will*

pass through the land of Egypt that night, and I will strike all the firstborn in the land of Egypt, both man and beast; and on all the gods of Egypt I will execute judgments: I am the Lord. ¹³ The blood shall be a sign for you, on the houses where you are. And when I see the blood, I will pass over you, and no plague will befall you to destroy you, when I strike the land of Egypt.

The response of the people is a response of faith—belief supported by action. They had deduced that if the other nine plagues happened, the tenth must be on its way also. So, each of them, Moses included, did as instructed. They took the innocent lamb, and they killed it. They captured the drained blood from the lamb, and they painted it on the door frame. Then, they roasted the lamb, and ate it as instructed.

There are a few things that I really appreciate about this chapter of Scripture. This Passover meal became the memorial meal of Israel, commemorating their salvation from the hand of Pharoah and the Egyptians. As you look a bit closer at the instructions given by God to Moses and by Moses to the people, you see that within the original instructions, there is a vision given that this meal would be memorialized for generations to come. It even says in Exodus 12:24-25:

You shall observe this rite as a statute for you and for your sons forever. ²⁵ And when you come to the land that the Lord will give you, as he has promised, you shall keep this service.

Notice with me the forward-looking faith of Moses as he instructs the people. As he is preparing them for this moment, he is also saying, "We aren't staying here any longer. Let's get ready to go."

In essences, the instruction is, "As you have received this rescue, you are going to pass this down from generation to generation. As you enter the promised land, you will also celebrate this sacrifice."

Now, notice Exodus 12:26-27. It states:

[26] And when your children say to you, 'What do you mean by this service?' [27] you shall say, 'It is the sacrifice of the Lord's Passover, for he passed over the houses of the people of Israel in Egypt, when he struck the Egyptians but spared our houses.' And the people bowed their heads and worshiped.

Notice the word, "sacrifice." From the very beginning, this moment has been understood as a sacrifice, the innocent lamb for the lives of the people. This application of the blood of the lambs on their doorposts is a forerunner to the blood of the Lamb of God, the Savior of the world, who spilled his blood for our salvation.

In 1878, Presbyterian minister, Elisha A. Hoffman wrote this song:

Are You Washed in the Blood?
Words & Music: Elisha A. Hoffman, 1878
Verse 1
Have you been to Jesus for the cleansing pow'r?
Are you washed in the blood of the Lamb?
Are you fully trusting in His grace this hour?
Are you washed in the blood of the Lamb?

Chorus

Are you washed in the blood,

In the soul-cleansing blood of the Lamb?

Are your garments spotless? Are they white as snow?

Are you washed in the blood of the Lamb?

Verse 2

Are you walking daily by the Savior's side?

Are you washed in the blood of the Lamb?

Do you rest each moment in the Crucified?

Are you washed in the blood of the Lamb?

Chorus

Verse 3

When the Bridegroom cometh will your robes be white?

Are you washed in the blood of the Lamb?

Will your soul be ready for the mansions bright,

And be washed in the blood of the Lamb?

Chorus

Verse 4

Lay aside the garments that are stained with sin,

And be washed in the blood of the Lamb;

There's a fountain flowing for the soul unclean,

O be washed in the blood of the Lamb![35]

My friend, are you washed in the blood of the Lamb? To be washed in the blood of the Lamb is to have your sin forgiven and washed away. To know that you are washed in the blood of the Lamb, the Lord Jesus, simply pray this prayer right now:

Lord Jesus, I know that I am a sinner in need of a Savior. I admit that I am condemned in my sin. I also believe that you are the Son of God who became a man and lived a perfect life. I believe that you died for me and that you rose again from the dead. I ask that you come into my life and save me. I call upon you today for my salvation. In your name, I pray, amen.

The night of the Passover was a dividing line between life and death—not because of anyone's status, wealth, or power, but because of the blood of the lamb. The same is true today. The only hope we have in life and in death is the blood of Jesus, our Passover Lamb. His sacrifice secures our salvation and shields us from the judgment we deserve. Faith applies that blood personally—trusting that His death and resurrection cover *my* sin

Prayer

Lord Jesus, thank You for being my Passover Lamb. Thank You that Your blood covers me, forgives me, and secures my place in the city You are preparing. Help me to live each day in the confidence of Your sacrifice and to share this good news with my family, friends, and neighbors. Keep me mindful that nothing else—no wealth, status, or effort of my own— can save me apart from You. Today, I choose to rest in Your blood, trust Your promises, and walk forward in faith. In Your holy name I pray, Amen.

FAITH IS...

Believing Judgement will Come

By faith he kept the Passover and sprinkled the blood, so that the Destroyer of the firstborn might not touch them.

HEBREWS 10:28

The story of Israel's exodus from Egypt is their nation's salvation story. As we have seen, it is one of drama and intrigue. After 400 years of growing as a people, and after many years of enslavement, God sends them Moses, a shepherd and deliverer, who grew up in the king's palace.

As Moses and Aaron work with the elders of the 12 tribes of Israel, it is clear that they have been sent by God. As noted yesterday, at the occurrence of the tenth plague, Moses warned Pharoah and also prepared the people.

They believed that the tenth plague was real, and in doing so, took the necessary action to apply the blood of the lamb to their doorposts. In taking this action, they were spared the judgment of the Angel of Death otherwise known as the Destroyer.

In this salvation story, you have those who hear and believe by acting in faith and those who hear, and do not believe. In this salvation story, you have those who are spared the judgment, and you have those who are not spared judgment. In this salvation story, you have those who are rescued from the oppressive king, and those who are destroyed because they served the oppressive regime.

The story of Exodus for Israel is a picture for all of the nations of what God is doing through Jesus Christ. Because mankind is in Adam, and has inherited Adam's sin nature, mankind is enslaved to sin, deceived by the oppressor, Satan.

Like the Exodus story, the salvation story through the gospel of Jesus, is one where people avoid judgment by placing their faith and trust in Jesus for the salvation of their souls. But the judgment isn't just the death of a firstborn. Instead, it is eternal condemnation for all of eternity.

The Scripture describes this place of judgment as Hell. The Baker Encyclopedia of the Bible defines Hell as, "Place of future punishment for the lost, unrepentant, wicked dead."[36] For a broader definition, the Baker Encyclopedia of the Bible states:

"Hell is the final destiny of unbelievers and is variously described by the figures of a furnace of fire, eternal fire, eternal punishment (Mt 13:42, 50; 25:41, 46); outer darkness, the place of weeping and torment (8:12); eternal sin (Mk 3:29); the wrath of God (Rom 2:5); everlasting separation from the Lord, never to see the glory of his power (2 Thes 1:9); the bottomless pit (Rv 9:1, 11); continuous torment (14:10, 11); the lake of fire, the second death (21:8); a place for the devil and his demons (Mt 25:41). The foregoing designations clearly show that the state of those in hell is one of eternal duration."[37]

Because of our identity as Adam's offspring, we needed one who was not born of Adam's seed to come and rescue us. Just like those who were aligned with Pharoah also suffered the consequence or Pharoah's choices, those who are aligned with the Devil, and those who fail to take action by taking Christ as their savior, will also experience the same fate of the Devil – eternal torment.

In March of 1748, John Newton, a rebellious sailor and slave trader, found himself caught in a violent storm off the coast of Ireland. As the ship was breaking apart, he cried out to God for mercy—something he had not done in years. Later that night, as he pumped water out of the sinking vessel, he remembered the words of Scripture his mother had taught him as a boy.

Newton would later look back on that night as the turning point of his life—the moment when he first responded in faith to God's call and escaped eternal judgment. Though his full conversion and growth in Christ would unfold over time, that storm marked the beginning of his rescue, both physically from the sea and spiritually from sin. Newton would go on to write the hymn *Amazing Grace*, testifying to God's mercy in saving "a wretch like me."[38]

Faith not only looks to God's promises of blessing but also takes seriously His warnings of judgment. The Israelites believed God's word, acted in faith, and were spared. Pharaoh hardened his heart, ignored the warning, and faced destruction. The same choice stands before us today. To reject Christ is to face eternal separation from God. To trust Him is to be covered by the blood of the Lamb and spared from judgment. Friend, do not take lightly what God has said. Believe His word, apply His blood, and walk in the freedom of salvation. Today, take a moment to examine your heart and ask: *Have I trusted fully in Christ for rescue? And am I urging others to escape judgment by pointing them to Jesus?*

Prayer

Lord, I believe that Your Word is true—both in its promises and in its warnings. Thank You for sending Jesus, the Lamb of God, to take away my sin and rescue me from judgment. Help me to live with urgency, not wasting my days, but pointing others to the only hope that saves. Keep me mindful of eternity, Lord, and give me courage to share the good news of Jesus with those still in danger of perishing. May my faith be marked by gratitude, holiness, and a burden for the lost. In Jesus' name, Amen.

FAITH IS...

A Gift We Give Back to God

By faith the people crossed the Red Sea as on dry land, but the Egyptians, when they attempted to do the same, were drowned.

HEBREWS 11:29

Barbara Snyder was diagnosed with multiple sclerosis (MS) in her teens and by the 1980s was in the final stages of the disease. She had been confined to her home and then hospice care for years, blind in one eye, unable to breathe without a ventilator, and curled in a fetal position from muscle contractions. Doctors declared her case terminal.

On Pentecost Sunday, June 1981, over 400 people who knew Barbara were praying for her healing. That day, she suddenly heard a voice, not audible to others, that said, *"My child, get up and walk!"* Immediately, she ripped the oxygen tube from her nose, stood up, and walked without assistance. Her atrophied muscles instantly regained strength. Doctors, nurses, and family witnessed her recovery. Barbara went on to live a normal, healthy life for decades, baffling medical professionals.

Her healing was so extraordinary that it was later documented in Craig Keener's scholarly work *Miracles: The Credibility of the New Testament Accounts* (Baker Academic, 2011), where it is cited as one of the most medically verified modern miracles.[39]

As Moses is leading the Hebrew people out of Egypt, he is being led by the cloud by day and fire by night. As he and the people follow, the Lord leads them all to the edge of the Red Sea, then the Lord turned them around to give the appearance that they were lost and walking in circles. Can you imagine the thought process happening in Moses' mind as they inched closer with every step to the sea? I am sure he was thinking, "God, what are you going to do here?"

The people were marked by fear, and they began to want to go back to being enslaved once again. Exodus 14:12-13 states:

> *Is not this what we said to you in Egypt: 'Leave us alone that we may serve the Egyptians'? For it would have been better for us to serve the Egyptians than to die in the wilderness.*

When fear marks our lives, we fail to see clearly. We lose sight of God's deliverance and provision in the past and we want to go back to something far less than ideal instead of pursuing God's vision for our future.

Now, notice the contrast of the people's mindset and Moses' confidence in God. Exodus 14:13-14 states:

And Moses said to the people, "Fear not, stand firm, and see the salvation of the Lord, which he will work for you today. For the Egyptians whom you see today, you shall never see again. ¹⁴ The Lord will fight for you, and you have only to be silent."

Note something with me before we see the entire nation cross on dry ground. The people lacked faith in this moment. They were ruled by fear. Their backs were against the wall, and they could see the enemy breathing down on them.

It is their new shepherd and leader, Moses, who has faith. He is the one saying, "The Lord will fight for you..." Moses' faith was stirred, and he invited the entire nation to not fear, but to stand firm and see the salvation of the Lord. And it was his faith that God honored to get all of them across on dry ground.

As you read the next verse, Moses tells the people to stand firm and be quiet but notice what the Lord says to him. Exodus 14:15-16 states:

The Lord said to Moses, "Why do you cry to me? Tell the people of Israel to go forward. ¹⁶ Lift up your staff, and stretch out your hand over the sea and divide it, that the people of Israel may go through the sea on dry ground.

Moses was confident that God was going to do something. Yet it also appears that the Lord is giving him a "C" on this exam. In one way, he did good. He positioned the people to lure in the Egyptians, and he was confident that they would see God move. But it is also here that Moses gets the next steps incorrect.

The Lord wanted the people to be moving toward the peril, not being held still by fear. He wanted Moses to not have the people just sit back in silence and wait, but to take action toward a way of escape, believing that God would do something miraculous.

To help us here, let's go back to Mark six when Jesus is in his own hometown, Nazareth. We looked at this on Day 19, from Matthew's gospel. It is here, the people listen and are moved by his teaching. They begin to say, "Hey, we know this guy. He is Joseph's son, and we know his mom and brothers. Who does he think he is?"

If you read it closely, you see them start their questions off speaking of his power and his authority to teach but quickly conclude that there is no way that he can be trusted or followed because they knew him when he was a kid.

Mark 6:4 then states:

⁴ And Jesus said to them, "A prophet is not without honor, except in his hometown and among his relatives and in his own household."

As Mark finishes this story, notice the commentary he gives as he writes his gospel. Mark 6:5-6 states:

And he could do no mighty work there, except that he laid his hands on a few sick people and healed them. ⁶ And he marveled because of their unbelief.

The Son of God was limited in that region because of their lack of faith. Moses had faith. He didn't get an "A" on the exam, but it was enough for God to work with, as all that is required is faith the size of a mustard-seed.

Do you believe in God's ability to heal, provide, rescue, set free, and restore? Does God still heal disease or deliver those whose back is against the wall? Has our western mindset limited God's ability in our region to do the miraculous?

Faith is God's gift to us, but it's also the one gift we can give back to Him. The Israelites had no strategy, no strength, and no way out when their backs were to the Red Sea—but by faith, they stepped forward, and God parted the waters. The same is true for us. When fear surrounds us, faith is what honors God and invites Him to move. Like Barbara Snyder rising from her sickbed or Moses raising his staff, faith positions us to see the miraculous. Will you give your faith back to God today? Take that next step of obedience, no matter how daunting. Offer Him trust instead of fear, movement instead of paralysis, and expectation instead of doubt.

Prayer

Lord, thank You for the gift of faith. Today, I give it back to You. I confess the places where fear has ruled my heart and where unbelief has limited my steps. Strengthen me to walk forward into the unknown, believing You will part the waters before me. Stir in me a mustard-seed faith that trusts Your power to heal, restore, and deliver. May my faith be my gift of worship, pleasing to You and a testimony to others that You are the God who still works wonders. In Jesus' name, Amen.

FAITH IS...

Persistent Obedience

*By faith the walls of Jericho fell down after they had been
encircled for seven days.*

HEBREWS 11:30

The children of Israel were commanded to do something unusual in their conquest of Jericho. God told them to march around the city once each day for six days, and then seven times on the seventh day. It wasn't a military strategy — it was a test of faith.

As the writer of Hebrews moves on from Moses' leadership, we pick up with Joshua and the fact that he and the Israelites have crossed over the Jordan river on dry ground, even though the river was at flood stage. They have settled their camp in Canaan, and now, they are on the move to conquer Jericho.

Jericho, this ancient city, is believed to be the oldest city in the world. Archaeology tells us that ancient Jericho was a fortified city with two massive walls. It had an inner wall about 12 feet thick and an outer wall about six feet thick.[40] I wonder if the spies who had entered the land 40 years prior had chronicled the thickness of the walls, adding to their unbelief that Jericho wasn't a city that could be conquered.

As this new generation of the Israelites enter the region, the book of Joshua notes that the entire city of Jericho has been closed, because the people of Jericho are captured with fear. Joshua 6:1-2 states:

> Now Jericho was shut up inside and outside because of the people of Israel. None went out, and none came in. ² And the Lord said to Joshua, "See, I have given Jericho into your hand, with its king and mighty men of valor."

The city itself covered about 6–9 acres, roughly the size of 6 or 7 football fields. Scholars estimate the circumference of the city was around 2,000–2,400 feet — just over half a mile.[41] That means one lap around Jericho was less than a mile.

Notice the instruction from the Lord to Joshua in Joshua 6:3-7:

> You shall march around the city, all the men of war going around the city once. Thus shall you do for six days. ⁴ Seven priests shall bear seven trumpets of rams' horns before the ark. On the seventh day you shall march around the city seven times, and the priests shall blow the trumpets. ⁵ And when they make a long blast with the ram's horn, when you hear the sound of the trumpet, then all the people shall shout with a

great shout, and the wall of the city will fall down flat, and the people shall go up, everyone straight before him." ⁶ *So Joshua the son of Nun called the priests and said to them, "Take up the ark of the covenant and let seven priests bear seven trumpets of rams' horns before the ark of the Lord."* ⁷ *And he said to the people, "Go forward. March around the city and let the armed men pass on before the ark of the Lord."*

So, here's the picture. As they start out from camp, the men of war are leading the way. After them, there are seven priests who will be blowing seven trumpets of rams' horns. After the priests, the ark of the Lord. After the ark of the Lord, the rear guard. After that, the people.

Before we move on from here, I want you to note something with me. The focus in Joshua 6 is about the ark of the Lord, which signifies God's presence. Subsequent to the ark is the people's obedience to the instructions. At least, that is how I read it. God's presence in the fight was the difference maker.

Now, notice the call to be obedient and persist in it. Joshua 6:10-14 states:

But Joshua commanded the people, "You shall not shout or make your voice heard, neither shall any word go out of your mouth, until the day I tell you to shout. Then you shall shout." ¹¹ *So he caused the ark of the Lord to circle the city, going about it once. And they came into the camp and spent the night in the camp.*

12 Then Joshua rose early in the morning, and the priests took up the ark of the Lord. 13 And the seven priests bearing the seven trumpets of rams' horns before the ark of the Lord walked on, and they blew the trumpets continually. And the armed men were walking before them, and the rear guard was walking after the ark of the Lord, while the trumpets blew continually. 14 And the second day they marched around the city once, and returned into the camp. So they did for six days.

For six days, Israel walked about 0.6 miles per day. On the seventh day, they marched about 4.2 miles in total — still very doable for families, soldiers, and priests. Altogether, across the whole week, they covered about 7–8 miles.

The true victory wasn't found in their fighting skills, but rather in their willingness to keep walking. On the seventh day, they were instructed to march seven times, and then, at the sound of the long trumpet, they were to shout to the Lord, and as the song declares, "... and the walls came tumblin' down!"

Faith that pleases God doesn't always look flashy. Sometimes it looks like showing up, day after day, repeating the same small steps of obedience that feel routine or even foolish. The Israelites' march around Jericho wasn't about military strength—it was about trust. God is honored when His people keep walking, keep praying, keep serving, and keep believing, even when the results aren't immediate. That's persistent obedience. And it's in persistence that the walls eventually fall. What walls in your life require you to keep circling in faith? Don't give up on the sixth day. Don't quit before the shout. Stay the course and watch what God will do.

Prayer

Lord, thank You for reminding me that obedience is often about persistence in the little things. Forgive me for the times I've grown weary and wanted to quit when the results weren't immediate. Strengthen me to keep walking in faith, even when it feels repetitive or strange. Help me trust that You are at work in ways I cannot see. Lord, bring down the walls in my life, and may my obedience bring glory to Your name. In Jesus' name, Amen.

FAITH IS...

Receiving a New Future

By faith Rahab the prostitute did not perish with those who
were disobedient, because she had given a friendly welcome
to the spies.

HEBREWS 11:31

Chrissy Outlaw grew up in a broken home and endured abuse from an early age. As a teenager she longed for love and affirmation but instead found herself trapped in toxic relationships. By her twenties, she became involved in the pornography industry, which promised quick money but left her feeling degraded and hopeless. She later said she felt like she was "too far gone" for God to forgive her.

But in 2003, Chrissy encountered Christians who loved her without judgment and told her that Jesus offered forgiveness and new life. She gave her life to Christ, walked away from the porn industry, and began a ministry sharing her testimony to help others find freedom in Christ. Like Rahab, her past did not disqualify her — instead, God redeemed her story to draw others to Himself. Today she has spoken at churches and conferences, telling thousands that no one is beyond God's grace.[42]

How does the gospel transform a life like this? How can a young woman go from a broken family, abuse in toxic relationships, and the pornography industry, to speaking in church and pointing people to hope?

I think the answer is simple: faith in Christ Jesus. The good news of Jesus changes our identity. Through Christ, we are moved from death to life, from darkness to light, and from enemies of God to children of God and co-heirs with Christ. Our Heavenly Father adopts us and grants us an inheritance, even though we were his enemies. This comes to us when we see the truth and respond in faith.

This is Rahab's story. Rahab was a prostitute living in Jericho when Israel came to conquer the city (Joshua 2). She hid two Israelite spies on her roof and misdirected the king's men who were searching for them. Rahab had heard of Israel's God — how He had parted the Red Sea and defeated mighty kings — and she confessed her faith. Joshua 2:8-14 states:

> *Before the men lay down, she came up to them on the roof[9] and said to the men, "I know that the Lord has given you the land, and that the fear of you has fallen upon us, and that all the inhabitants of the land melt away before you. [10] For we have heard how the Lord dried up the water of the Red Sea*

before you when you came out of Egypt, and what you did to the two kings of the Amorites who were beyond the Jordan, to Sihon and Og, whom you devoted to destruction. ¹¹And as soon as we heard it, our hearts melted, and there was no spirit left in any man because of you, for the Lord your God, he is God in the heavens above and on the earth beneath. ¹²Now then, please swear to me by the Lord that, as I have dealt kindly with you, you also will deal kindly with my father's house, and give me a sure sign ¹³that you will save alive my father and mother, my brothers and sisters, and all who belong to them, and deliver our lives from death." ¹⁴And the men said to her, "Our life for yours even to death! If you do not tell this business of ours, then when the Lord gives us the land we will deal kindly and faithfully with you."

Because of her faith, she asked the spies to spare her family. She took courageous action to secure the rescue of her entire family because of what she could see coming. Thus, the spies promised safety if she tied a scarlet cord in her window as a sign.

Before we move on from this scarlet cord, consider a few nuggets of deeper meaning:

"The scarlet cord tied in Rahab's window held significant meaning in the story of Jericho's fall. It served as a symbol of salvation for Rahab and her family, marking her house for protection when the Israelites conquered the city.[43][44] This cord was part of an agreement between Rahab and the Israelite spies, requiring her to keep her family inside the house during the attack. The scarlet color of the cord has been interpreted by many Christian scholars as a foreshadowing of Christ's blood and sacrifice.[45] [46] Rahab's act of hanging the cord was seen as a public declaration of her faith.[47] Her story is notable not only for her salvation but also for her subsequent integration into Israelite society and her place in the lineage of Jesus Christ.[48] The scarlet cord in Rahab's story is often compared to the blood-marked doorposts during the first Passover in Egypt, both serving as signs of divine protection."[49] [50]

What riches we find in the word of God! When the walls of Jericho fell, Rahab and her household were spared (Joshua 6:22–25). This set Rahab apart from the rest of Jericho and gave her a new future.

Rahab's story shows that faith, not background, secures salvation. Even a Canaanite prostitute can become part of God's covenant people through belief. As you ponder this truth, consider also how Rahab was the mother of Boaz and the great-great-grandmother of King David. She even appears in Matthew's gospel as part of the lineage of Jesus.

Rahab's scarlet cord still speaks to us today—it points us to the blood of Jesus, which secures our salvation and gives us a brand-new future. Your past does not disqualify you. Your mistakes do not define you. By faith, you too can be marked by the blood of Christ and welcomed into God's family. Just as Rahab's household was spared and Chrissy Outlaw's life was transformed, so can yours. Faith is not about where you've been, but about who you trust now. Will you place your full confidence in Jesus and receive the future He has prepared for you?

Prayer

Father, thank You that Your grace is greater than my past. Thank You for the scarlet cord that points me to the blood of Jesus, shed for my forgiveness. I confess that I need You to redeem my story and give me a new future. Help me to live by faith, trusting You to protect, guide, and restore me. Use my life as a testimony of Your transforming love. In Jesus' name, Amen.

FAITH IS...

Fundamental to Godly Leadership

And what more shall I say? For time would fail me to tell
of Gideon, Barak, Samson, Jephthah, of David and Samuel
and the prophets—

HEBREWS 11:32

Do you feel the story picking up steam? As you read Hebrews 11, you begin to jump through Israel's history, as if the writer is skipping a rock over the book of Judges, the kings and the prophets. Hundreds of years are covered in these two sentences.

So, what are we to note? I think it's right back to what we saw as we opened Hebrews 11 – "Without faith, it is impossible to please God."

Why are these leaders mentioned when others aren't? Where is King Saul? He was the first king of Israel. Why is King David mentioned and not Saul? David wasn't perfect.

Is Samson really worthy of mentioning? Barak? Didn't Barak hesitate and the glory go to Deborah? Jephthah was a fierce warrior and one who made a rash vow that cost him the life of his only daughter. Does he really fit the hall of faith?

It's interesting to consider a quick summation of the lives of these leaders and see a lot of brokenness. After leading Israel to victory, Gideon, resisted leadership and being made king, then named his son, Abimelech, which means, son of the king. It seems it was a false humility.

Samson was motivated by pleasure. He didn't fear God. He toyed with temptation and succumbed. Yet at the end of his days, God still used him, in a moment when he cried out in faith. David was mighty in faith, then strayed, committing adultery with Bathsheba and having her husband killed.

These leaders weren't perfect; rather, they were far from it. So, why are they mentioned here?

I am going to share with you the verses that follow, though in the days ahead, we will still mine these verses for principles of faith. But notice the rest of the sentence from the writer of Hebrews in Hebrews 11:32-34:

And what more shall I say? For time would fail me to tell of Gideon, Barak, Samson, Jephthah, of David and Samuel and the prophets— [33] who through faith conquered kingdoms, enforced justice, obtained promises, stopped the mouths of lions, [34] quenched the power of fire, escaped the edge of the sword, were made strong out of weakness, became mighty in war, put foreign armies to flight.

Each of these are noted for their faith and how when deployed at a moment in time, their journeys created blessing, rescue, salvation, and rest for others. They get included in the hall of faith, not for living perfect lives, but because in a moment of crises, as leaders, they stood in faith, and it changed the course of Israel's story.

This is often how we view our political leaders as well. Abraham Lincoln, America's 16th president, was far from a perfect man. He battled lifelong depression, wrestled with doubts, and came from humble, unpolished beginnings. Politically, he was often ridiculed, underestimated, and even despised. Yet in the darkest days of the Civil War, when the nation was fractured and the Union's survival was in question, Lincoln demonstrated remarkable leadership rooted in faith and moral courage.

In 1862, as pressure mounted and voices around him urged compromise with slavery to restore peace, Lincoln instead issued the Emancipation Proclamation — declaring freedom for slaves in Confederate territory. He admitted to his cabinet that he made the decision "after much prayer"[51] and that he had promised God that if the Union won a major victory (which came at Antietam), he would move forward with emancipation.

Lincoln's action was not politically safe. It was divisive, unpopular in many parts of the North, and risky in terms of military strategy. Yet his stand of faith and conviction transformed the war from simply a battle to preserve the Union into a moral crusade for human freedom. This decision changed the trajectory of the war, inspired enslaved people, bolstered Union morale, and reshaped the very identity of America.

As historian Allen Guelzo notes: "Lincoln's act of emancipation was an act of faith...he had no guarantees it would succeed, but he trusted that God's justice demanded it and that the Union cause would be vindicated."[52]

If you are responsible for others, as a parent, teacher, employer, coach, or bus driver, remember, you won't be perfect. As a matter of fact, in leading others, you recognize how far from perfect you are. But just because you won't be perfect, doesn't mean that you should give up the fight. Instead, cultivate your faith. Grow your understanding of God and his ways and make faith a fundamental part of your leadership journey. In doing so, God will bless you, and more importantly, those you lead.

Prayer

Father, I confess that I often feel inadequate as a leader. I see my flaws and wonder if You can use me. Thank You for reminding me through Your Word that You use broken vessels who place their faith in You. Strengthen me to lead with conviction, courage, and humility. When I face difficult choices, help me to choose what honors You, even when it's costly. Let my faith be a blessing to those I lead. In Jesus' name, Amen.

FAITH IS...

the Catalyst to Advance, and the Strength to Stand Fast

who through faith conquered kingdoms, enforced justice,
obtained promises, stopped the mouths of lions, quenched the
power of fire, escaped the edge of the sword...

HEBREWS 11:33-34A

During World War II, one of the most unlikely heroes wore no weapon on his side. His name was Desmond Doss, a devout Christian who, because of his faith, refused to carry a gun. A conscientious objector, he enlisted not to take life but to save it—as a combat medic.

The ridicule was relentless. Fellow soldiers mocked him, branded him a coward, and even threatened his life. Yet Doss kept showing up—through training, through abuse, through the long stretches of isolation. Quietly, he held to his conviction: "While others are taking life, I'll be saving it."

That conviction was tested at the Battle of Okinawa in 1945. As bullets ripped through the air and men fell by the dozens, Doss didn't retreat. Instead, he scaled the sheer cliffs of "Hacksaw Ridge," and then—repeatedly—he went back into the fire to pull the wounded out.

By nightfall, he had lowered 75 men to safety, one at a time. With each rescue, he prayed the same simple prayer: "Lord, let me get one more."

Doss's devotion was not loud or glamorous. It was steady, unseen, and costly. But when it mattered most, he kept showing up. His courage earned him the Medal of Honor—the first ever awarded to a conscientious objector.[53]

In Doss, we have the example of faith that enabled one to both take a stand and advance a mission forward. As we look at the group of leaders like Gideon, Barak, Samson, David and the others noted in verse 32, we see that it was this same faith that enabled them to both advance God's purposes and endure severe persecution.

Notice those whose faith helped them advance God's purposes. These are Joshua, the Judges, and King David, as they conquered kingdoms. David and Solomon who ruled in a way to enforce justice. Abraham walked forward and obtained God's promise of Isaac. But there is another who conquered kingdoms, who is worthy of our attention. He too, scaled some hills. That man is Caleb.

At 85 years old, Caleb boldly claimed the hill country of Hebron, the very land where the dreaded Anakim giants lived. While others shrank back at their size and strength, Caleb's faith in God's promise never wavered. Look at his declaration in Joshua 14:10–12:

> "And now, behold, the LORD has kept me alive, just as he said, these forty-five years since the time that the LORD spoke this word to Moses... And now, behold, I am this day eighty-five years old. I am still as strong today as I was in the day that Moses sent me; my strength now is as my strength was then, for war and for going and coming. So now give me this hill country of which the LORD spoke on that day, for you heard on that day how the Anakim were there, with great fortified cities. It may be that the LORD will be with me, and I shall drive them out just as the LORD said." (ESV)

With God's help, Caleb drove out the giants Sheshai, Ahiman, and Talmai, securing Hebron as his inheritance—a lasting testimony that wholehearted faith can conquer even the most intimidating obstacles (Joshua 14:6–15; 15:13–14).

Now let's spend a minute talking about how faith served to help these persevere and endure. These are those who, "...stopped the mouths of lions, quenched the power of fire, escaped the edge of the sword..." Faith not only allows us to move forward, but it also helps us stand and remain.

It was Daniel in the den of lions, and his three friends, Shadrach, Meshach, and Abednego, in the fiery furnace, that all escaped certain deaths because they were willing to take a stand for the glory of God. God honored their faith and delivered them. Elijah, Elisha, and David escaped the edge of the sword, escaping evil leaders who sought to take their lives.

All of these placed together could be put on display as a team picture in the hall of faith, where some were playing offense and some defense. It is in this picture that the writer of Hebrews is stacking together a gallery of faith-heroes to show that God delivered His people in miraculous ways when they trusted Him.

Remember, faith is not passive—it compels us both to advance when God calls and to stand firm when trials come. Sometimes faith looks like Caleb charging the hills at 85, or Desmond Doss crawling back into the fire to save one more life. Other times, it looks like Daniel kneeling in prayer despite a decree, or Shadrach, Meshach, and Abednego standing tall before a furnace. Whether advancing or enduring, faith fixes its eyes on God and trusts Him for the outcome. Where is God calling you to move forward today? And where is He asking you to stand fast in quiet trust?

Prayer

Father, give me the faith to discern when to march forward and when to stand firm. Strengthen me to face the "giants" before me and the "fires" around me with confidence in Your power. Teach me to trust Your timing, Your promises, and Your deliverance. May my faith not shrink back but instead be a testimony to Your glory. In Jesus' name, Amen.

FAITH IS...

Believing Strength Comes from Weakness

...were made strong out of weakness...

HEBREWS 11:34B

You may have heard the phrase, "What doesn't kill you makes you stronger." Glenn Cunningham's story certainly relates to this. During the 1930s, as a young boy, Glenn was caught in a horrific schoolhouse fire. His legs were so badly burned that doctors recommended amputation. They told his parents he would never walk again. But Glenn refused to accept it. With braces, crutches, and fierce determination, he began the long, painful process of retraining his legs to move.

What seemed like the end of his life became the very stage for God's strength. Glenn not only walked, but he also ran. He ran so well that he went on to set the world record for the mile in 1934 and competed in two Olympic Games, earning the nickname *"The Kansas Ironman."* From a hospital bed of weakness to the world's fastest man, Glenn's story reminds us that God can turn our weakest moments into a testimony of strength.[54]

Has God ever done that for you? My mile time isn't getting faster, that's for sure, but I have seen God bring something powerful out of situations where I was completely helpless. As you look through the testimony of Scripture, this seems to be a common theme.

Consider Samson. Samson was set apart from his birth as a Nazarite. This vow gave him to the Lord and as a sign of it, he was not to cut his hair, drink wine, or touch any unclean thing. Samson also experienced the Spirit of the Lord coming upon him in extraordinary ways, enabling feats of supernatural strength (Judges 14:6; 15:14–15). He tore apart a lion with his bare hands, struck down a thousand Philistines with the jawbone of a donkey, and carried away the gates of Gaza on his shoulders (Judges 16:3).

But Samson is also remembered as a deeply flawed judge of Israel. He was impulsive, often acting on raw emotion rather than wisdom, as when he demanded a Philistine wife simply because she pleased him (Judges 14:2–3). He was lustful and sexually immoral, pursuing women outside God's covenant people, including a prostitute (Judges 16:1) and Delilah (Judges 16:4). He was proud and arrogant, boasting in his own strength and forgetting that it was the Spirit of the Lord who empowered him (Judges 15:16). His actions were often driven by revenge rather than by a righteous desire to deliver Israel (Judges

15:7–8). Though set apart as a Nazarite, he was disobedient to his vows, touching dead bodies (Judges 14:8–9), drinking at feasts, and finally revealing the secret of his strength to Delilah (Judges 16:17). He was also foolish and easily deceived, ignoring repeated betrayals until Delilah finally delivered him to the Philistines (Judges 16:6–21). Undisciplined and reckless, Samson wasted much of his God-given gift of strength through careless living instead of consistent faithfulness.

This careless living landed him in a Philistine prison where he was tortured, and his eyes were gouged out. Yet, in this place, God met Samson there. His final act of faith came in weakness, when blinded and humiliated, he prayed for strength one last time and brought down the Philistine temple, striking a decisive blow against Israel's oppressors (Judges 16:28–30). Though inconsistent, Samson's story testifies that God can use even deeply flawed individuals to accomplish His purposes and that true strength is found not in human might but in dependence on the Lord.

Beyond Samson, as you read in the New Testament, the Apostle Paul actually relishes his weaknesses. In his own defense of his apostleship, he opens chapter 12 of 2 Corinthians, stating that he has every reason to boast as an Apostle. It appears he even is referring to himself, when in chapter 12, he talks about a man he knew that had gone to the third heaven and had been given revelations that were unspeakable. Notice then what he says about a thorn in his flesh.

2 Corinthians 12:7b-9 states:

Therefore, in order to keep me from becoming conceited, I was given a thorn in my flesh, a messenger of Satan, to torment me. ⁸ Three times I pleaded with the Lord to take it away from me. ⁹ But he said to me, "My grace is sufficient for you, for my power is made perfect in weakness." Therefore I will boast all the more gladly about my weaknesses, so that Christ's power may rest on me.

The irony here is that both Samson and the Apostle Paul learned the same thing – the truth that God's power is made perfect in weakness. One man was so arrogant, he put himself in the predicament to come to the end of himself and ask for help. The other man was prevented from becoming arrogant through some sort of trial or suffering. Yet, both men learned the same truth.

Faith doesn't deny weakness—it embraces it as the very place where God shows up. Glenn Cunningham, Samson, and Paul each remind us that our frailty is not the end of the story. In fact, it's often the beginning of God's greatest work in us. What weakness are you carrying today—physical, emotional, relational, or spiritual? Instead of hiding it or despising it, bring it before the Lord. Ask Him to turn your weakness into strength, so that His power may rest on you.

Prayer

Father, I confess my weakness before You today. I don't want to rely on my own strength, which fails me, but on Yours, which never runs dry. Teach me to boast in my weakness so that Christ's power may rest on me. Where I feel empty, fill me with Your Spirit. Where I feel helpless, strengthen me with Your grace. Use my frailty as a stage for Your glory. In Jesus' name, Amen.

FAITH IS...

Becoming Mighty in the War

...became mighty in war, put foreign armies to flight.

HEBREWS 11:34C

One of the most haunting stories in the history of exploration is that of Robert Falcon Scott, the British naval officer who led the Terra Nova Expedition to the South Pole in 1910–1912. Scott was driven, courageous, and brilliant, but he was also stubborn and often ignored advice. Instead of using dogs like the Norwegians, he insisted on man-hauling sledges and even brought ponies, which quickly died in the Antarctic cold.

Scott's rival, Roald Amundsen, carefully prepared, embraced proven methods, and reached the South Pole first in December 1911. When Scott and his men finally arrived a month later, they found the Norwegian flag already planted. Defeated and discouraged, they began the long return trek. Supplies dwindled, morale collapsed, and one by one the men gave up. The last entries in Scott's journal reveal despair, exhaustion, and resignation. They were just 11 miles from a supply depot when they stopped and never moved again.[55]

Scott had the talent, the resources, and the opportunity to make history. Instead, by failing to persevere, he became a tragic warning of unfulfilled potential. His story reminds us that quitting short of the finish line means never experiencing the fullness of what could have been.[56]

In Hebrews 11:34c, the writer of Hebrews points us to people who were considered weak by human standards. Whether they were outnumbered like Gideon, or Jonathan and his armor-bearer, or small in stature like David when he faced Goliath, the odds were stacked against them.

In both stories, there were vast numbers who could go into battle. In the story of David and Goliath, Israel's army was lined up on one side of the Valley of Elah. King Saul was there, as were all the fighting men of Israel. Yet every man was afraid and remained so for 40 days.

In the story of Gideon leading Israel against the Midianites, there were up to 22,000 who could have gone to fight with him. Yet, the Lord would not have gotten glory if this had been the fighting force.

The Lord said to Gideon, in Judges 7:2, "The people with you are too many for me to give the Midianites into their hand, lest Israel boast over me, saying, 'My own hand has saved me.'" If you recall the story, there were two phases of paring down the numbers until it was Gideon with 300 men. God intentionally placed Gideon and the fighting men in their weakness so that they would have to depend on Him. He did this for his glory and credit.

When David showed up to the battle lines to give his brothers bread and cheese and to take a word of their well-being back to his father, he stepped onto the battlefield in weakness. He wasn't the experienced fighting man with the armor, size, and strength of Goliath.

In both cases, it was the Lord who made them mighty in the fight. Their faith was one where they believed that God was bigger than anything that life could throw at them. Though out-manned and out-gunned, they believed God was able to do more than they could imagine. It was there, in the fight, in their weakness, while walking by faith, that they became mighty in war.

In the early 20th century, Helen Keller became one of the most inspiring figures in modern history. At 19 months old, she was struck by an illness—likely scarlet fever or meningitis—that left her both blind and deaf. For a young child in that era, it seemed like a life sentence of isolation. She was frustrated, uncontrollable, and unable to communicate with the world around her. Many doubted she would ever learn to function, let alone flourish.

Then came her teacher, Anne Sullivan, who broke through Helen's silence with persistence and creativity. The process was agonizing. For months Helen resisted, but Anne pressed on, spelling words into her hand, showing her objects, patiently connecting language to life. The breakthrough came when Anne pumped water over Helen's hand while spelling "w-a-t-e-r." In that moment, Helen realized that the shapes traced into her palm were words that named the world around her.[57]

From that point on, Helen's determination was unstoppable. She went on to graduate from Radcliffe College in 1904, becoming the first deaf-blind person to earn a Bachelor of Arts degree. She authored books, gave lectures around the world, and became a leading voice for people with disabilities. What could have been a life defined by defeat became a life marked by courage, resilience, and global influence.[58]

When we look at these stories—of Gideon and his 300 men, of David with only a sling, of Helen Keller with seemingly insurmountable challenges—we are reminded that faith is not the absence of weakness, but the willingness to trust God in the midst of it. Robert Falcon Scott teaches us what happens when we faint in adversity; Helen Keller shows us what can happen when we persevere. The writer of Hebrews reminds us that ordinary men and women, weak by every human standard, became mighty in war because they leaned on the power of God.

So, where are you tempted to faint today? Where are you considering giving up—on your calling, your marriage, your health, or your ministry? Remember this: faith doesn't deny weakness, but it surrenders weakness to God and keeps showing up. It is there, in your dependence on Him, that He makes you mighty. Don't stop short. Don't let quitting define your story. Trust God with your weakness, step back into the battle, and let Him make you mighty.

Prayer

Lord, I confess that too often I want to quit when life gets hard. I see my weakness and I lose heart. But today I choose to trust You. Where I am weak, make me strong in Your power. Where I feel outnumbered, remind me that You are greater. Help me persevere, and by faith, become mighty in the war You have called me to fight. In Jesus' name, Amen.

FAITH IS...

Knowing this Life is Not the End

Women received back their dead by resurrection. Some were
tortured, refusing to accept release, so that they might rise
again to a better life.

HEBREWS 11:35

Part of the fun of this journey together has been the walk through the stories of the Old Testament. We've gone back to the beginning, to Abel, the son of Adam and Eve, and as we have made it through these in the hall of faith, it's as if the writer of Hebrews is accelerating to the days of Jesus. His statements are now summations, referring to a few stories along the way, and getting his reader toward a crescendo of faith.

In verse 35, the resurrection of the dead is the fruit of faith. These women who received back their dead were the widow who served

Elijah from 1 Kings 17, and the Shunamite woman who served Elisha in 2 Kings 4, both receiving back their sons.

The second part of this verse speaks to those being tortured for their beliefs. Many believe that this section of the verse is widely understood to point to Jewish martyrs during the Maccabean period (2nd century BC). The clearest historical parallels are found in the Apocrypha, particularly 2 Maccabees 6–7, which recounts how the elderly scribe Eleazar was tortured to death for refusing to eat pork (2 Maccabees 6:18–31),[59] and how a mother and her seven sons were executed one by one by King Antiochus IV Epiphanes after refusing to renounce their faith and eat forbidden food (2 Maccabees 7:1–42).[60] Each of them faced death with hope in the resurrection, declaring that God would raise them to eternal life.[61]

As you look at the belief in the resurrection in the Old Testament, you see this belief in bits and pieces, starting with Hosea. One writer states, "The first specific mention of the hope of a resurrection is found in Hosea, where the prophet's words are rather of the nature of an aspiration than the distinct announcement of a future event (6:2, cf. 13:14)."[62] The Psalmists speak of it, Ezekiel's valley of dry bones conveys God's ability to bring resurrection forth, and Daniel most clearly articulates the doctrine of the resurrection in the Old Testament. Daniel 12: 2 states:

"And many of those who sleep in the dust of the earth shall awake, some to everlasting life, and some to shame and everlasting contempt."

As you speed to the time of Jesus, you see the emerging doctrine of the resurrection during this Maccabean period. These extra-biblical works don't clearly articulate a standard doctrine of the resurrection but instead convey a variety of views of it. The resurrection of the dead is written about in the Book of Enoch, the Psalms of Solomon, and 2 Maccabees.

In 2 Maccabees, one writer declares, "A very definite doctrine of the resurrection is taught in this book, though the author expressly denies its applicability to the Gentiles (7:14, cf. 2 Es 7 [79f]). The resurrection of the body is strongly held, as affording a powerful incentive and a glorious hope for those who underwent a cruel martyrdom (14:46, 7:11, cf. 7:9, 14)."[63]

By the time we get to the New Testament, we know that the Pharisees teach and embrace the resurrection of the dead, and that Martha, the sister of Lazarus believes deeply in the resurrection. John 11:24 states, "Martha said to him, 'I know that he will rise again in the resurrection on the last day.'" In Acts 23:6, the Apostle Paul declares that it is because of the belief in the resurrection that he is on trial. Acts 23:6 states, "Now when Paul perceived that one part were Sadducees and the other Pharisees, he cried out in the council, 'Brothers, I am a Pharisee, a son of Pharisees. It is with respect to the hope and the resurrection of the dead that I am on trial.'"

The point that I am making is the sense that the doctrine of the resurrection was ripening so that by the time of Jesus and his resurrection, the Christian church could preach that Jesus was the very resurrection and the life of God available to all humanity. The resurrection of Jesus is the cornerstone doctrine of our faith because, "if Christ has not been raised, your faith is futile and you are still in your sins," (1 Corinthians 15:17). It is this truth that we preach, stand upon, and celebrate. The reason we do this is because of the last part of Hebrews 11:35, which states, "...so that they might rise again to a better life."

The reason Jesus came to die was to conquer sin and death, and to bring us to God. The promise that God makes to us is that we will rise again to a better life. This better life—the city where God is the architect and maker—the new heaven, earth, and New Jerusalem, is what will enable the believer to both endure violent persecution, and severe hardship, which we will see in our final few days together.

In the meantime, the hope of the resurrection steadies us in the face of fear, loss, and even death itself. The women who received their sons back, the martyrs who endured torture, and the apostles who stood on trial all clung to this truth: this life is not the end. Because Jesus is risen, we too will rise to a better life with Him. That hope fuels courage, sustains endurance, and gives us strength to live faithfully in a world full of trials.

Today, fix your eyes on the risen Christ. Let the promise of resurrection give you courage to endure hardship, faith to stand firm, and joy in the face of suffering. Live with confidence that the best life—the better life—is yet to come.

Prayer

Lord Jesus, thank you that You are the resurrection and the life. Because You live, I have hope beyond the grave. Strengthen me when I am weak, steady me when I am afraid, and remind me daily that this life is not the end. Help me endure hardship with joy, and give me courage to share the hope of Your resurrection with others. I look forward to that better life in Your presence forever. Amen.

FAITH IS...

Being Faithful in the Face of Death

Others suffered mocking and flogging, and even chains and imprisonment. They were stoned, they were sawn in two, they were killed with the sword...

HEBREWS 11:36-37A

Just this week, at the time of this writing, I received an email that reads:

I pray this message finds you all well. I wanted to share something close to my heart. As you may know, there has been an ongoing campaign to raise awareness about the persecution of Christians in Eritrea and beyond. Believers there continue to face imprisonment, intimidation, and suffering simply for practicing their faith.

Among them are seven ministers who have now been imprisoned for two decades simply for leading their congregations. Their story is a reminder of the heavy price many pay to remain faithful.

I believe it is important for us, as part of the body of Christ, to remember them, pray for them, and create awareness among our church members and wider communities.[64]

Attached to this email were a number of resources focused on the country of Eritrea on the eastern coast of Africa, that is persecuting Christians. A 2025 report from the USCIRF states:

> As of May, over 350 Christians were imprisoned, including more than 80 whom authorities arrested during the first five months of the year. Another estimate places 10,000 prisoners of conscience of all types in over 300 facilities around the country. Government authorities targeted several communities, including Baptists, Pentecostals, and others, for persecution and arrest, calling them "agents of the West." As in prior years, the government encouraged community surveillance of nontraditional Protestant Christians, labeling them "unpatriotic." The state sometimes temporarily releases prisoners but re-arrests them if they do not renounce their faith and regularly report to authorities. Police at times arrest entire Christian families, including children, during the early morning hours. The month of May marked the 20th anniversary of the arrests of Pastors Kiflu Gebremeskel and Haile Naizghe, both associated with the banned Full Gospel Church of Eritrea.[65]

As you read these reports, you realize that so many of our brothers and sisters throughout the world are persecuted for their faith in Jesus. This persecution of followers of Jesus is nothing new. From the stoning of Stephen, the arrests of followers of the Way by Saul, as he zealously persecuted the church, to those who suffered under Roman persecution for much of the first three centuries, the tactics of those opposed to Jesus haven't changed much.

Consider The Martyrs of Abitinae (AD 304), whose confession was, "We Cannot Live Without Sunday."

During Emperor Diocletian's fierce persecution of Christians in the early 4th century, Roman law forbade gatherings for worship. In the town of Abitinae (modern-day Tunisia), a group of 49 Christians defied the decree by meeting secretly on Sunday to celebrate the Lord's Supper.

Soldiers stormed their gathering and dragged them before the governor. When interrogated about why they broke the imperial edict, their leader, Emeritus, answered simply, "Sine dominico non possumus," which means, "Without Sunday, we cannot live."

The governor mocked them, beat them, and demanded they renounce Christ. They refused. One by one, men and women, wealthy and poor, old and young, testified that their life had no meaning apart from worshiping Jesus.

They were tortured with whips, chains, and cruel imprisonment. Many were executed by the sword. Yet they died declaring that Christ was worth more than life itself.[66]

Or consider Blandina, one of the martyrs of Lyons and Vienne (AD 177, Gaul/France).

In southern France, Christians faced brutal persecution under Marcus Aurelius. Many were tortured publicly—flogged, burned, and exposed to wild beasts. A young slave-girl named Blandina was especially mocked for her weakness. Yet she endured whipping, roasting, and being thrown to animals, continually confessing: "I am a Christian, and nothing wicked is done among us." She finally died on the cross-shaped stake, a living picture of her Savior.[67]

How might you respond if you were arrested because the authorities learned you were a Christian? Would you stay faithful because you know what lies ahead is far better than what you possess today?

Faith like this both humbles and strengthens us. We are reminded that while our daily struggles may feel heavy, countless brothers and sisters around the world face imprisonment, torture, and even death simply for naming the name of Christ. Their courage calls us to deeper faith, to live boldly for Jesus in our own context, and to lift them up in prayer.

So today, take time to pray for the persecuted church. Pray for endurance, courage, and joy for those suffering for Christ's sake. Pray that their testimony would win many to Jesus. And pray also for your own faith—that God would strengthen you to stand firm in the face of trials, great or small.

Prayer

Lord, we lift up our persecuted brothers and sisters around the world. Strengthen their hearts, sustain their faith, and surround them with Your presence. Give them courage to endure and hope that cannot be taken away. And Father, strengthen my own faith. Help me to be bold, unashamed, and faithful—whether in small daily trials or in moments of greater cost. May my life, like theirs, declare that Christ is worth more than life itself. In Jesus' name, Amen.

FAITH IS...

Persevering Because Jesus is Better

They went about in skins of sheep and goats, destitute, afflicted, mistreated— of whom the world was not worthy— wandering about in deserts and mountains, and in dens and caves of the earth.

HEBREWS 11:37B-38

My thermostat is set to 74 degrees. It's a Sunday afternoon, and my wife is stretched out on the couch, taking a nap. I've been texting with a friend who is a Cowboys fan about the Micah Parsons trade, and he is absolutely devastated.

It's pretty comfortable in my house today. As I read our verses for today from Hebrews 11, it is hard to really grasp this sort of reality for brothers and sisters in Christ. Yet, this is the third day of one continuous thought about those who were persecuted for their faith, as laid out for us in Hebrews 11:36-38.

Did you know that these three verses are one sentence in the Greek? The writer has taken us from biblical examples of victory and resurrection, to suddenly walking us through painful persecution of the faithful remnant. This passage most likely refers to a mixture of figures: Old Testament prophets (especially Elijah, Elisha, and others who lived in poverty and isolation), David hiding in caves, and the Maccabean martyrs who fled to the wilderness and suffered for their faith.

The author of Hebrews is painting a broad portrait of faithful endurance in the face of mistreatment and exile, not necessarily identifying just one person. Notice something with me as we are nearing the finish line together in this 40-day devotional.

It says in verse 38, "...of whom the world was not worthy..." F.F. Bruce states, "the phrase *'of whom the world was not worthy'* is a striking reversal: the world despised them as worthless, but in God's sight, they were too good for the world."[68]

I love that perspective. The world discards the people of God, but God has not discarded the people of the world. Instead, He has continued to provide a faithful witness to each generation so that He can reach every single nation, tribe, and tongue.

In the Middle East today, countless believers live the very reality described in Hebrews. One powerful example comes from Christians in northern Iraq during the ISIS invasion of 2014. When ISIS forces swept into Mosul, they gave Christians three options: convert to Islam, pay an impossible tax, or die. Families who had lived in the Nineveh plains for centuries were driven from their homes with nothing but the clothes on their backs. Many fled into the desert and the mountains of Kurdistan. With no shelter, they took refuge in abandoned buildings, caves, or makeshift tents. Mothers cradled babies in the open air; the elderly limped along dusty roads; entire congregations carried crosses hidden beneath their garments.[69]

One survivor later told *Open Doors International*:

> "They painted the letter 'N' for Nazarene on our doors to mark us as Christians. They thought we were not worthy of our homes. But I realized — in God's eyes, they were not worthy of us, for we belong to Christ."[70]

This testimony echoes Hebrews 11:38 — *"of whom the world was not worthy."* While the world cast them out as unworthy, God saw them as His precious ones, worthy of eternal glory.

These displaced Christians lost homes, possessions, and safety, but they did not lose faith. Gathered in tents and refugee camps, they worshiped with lifted hands, still proclaiming Jesus as Lord. Their perseverance is a modern reminder that faith can survive when stripped of every earthly comfort because knowing and following Jesus is better than anything this world has to offer.

The world may strip us of possessions, opportunities, or even safety, but it cannot take away Christ. Will you pray again today for persecuted believers—those living in deserts, tents, or secret caves—

who continue to hold fast to Jesus? Will you also ask God to give you the same faith, so that if your comforts are stripped away, you will still cling to Him?

Prayer

Lord, strengthen Your church around the world—especially those cast out of homes, wandering in deserts and mountains, or hiding in caves because they bear Your name. Make their faith unshakable and let their witness shine in the darkness. Strengthen me also, that I may hold fast to You even if the world turns against me. May I live as one "of whom the world is not worthy." In Jesus' name, Amen.

FAITH IS...

Knowing Something Better is Coming

And all these, though commended through their faith, did not receive what was promised, since God had provided something better for us, that apart from us they should not be made perfect.

HEBREWS 11:39-40

Former NFL quarterback and Dallas Theological Seminary Professor Dr. David Klinger answered this question posed of him, very succinctly. The question was, "How were the people of the Old Testament saved?" His answer was simple: "They placed their faith in the one who was to come. We have placed our faith in the one who came."

The entire theme of the book of Hebrews is the supremacy of Jesus Christ and how He is better. These in the hall of faith are now the ones surrounding us as the cloud of witnesses. Hebrews 12:1-2 states:

> *Therefore, since we are surrounded by so great a cloud of witnesses, let us also lay aside every weight, and sin which clings so closely, and let us run with endurance the race that is set before us, ² looking to Jesus, the founder and perfecter of our faith, who for the joy that was set before him endured the cross, despising the shame, and is seated at the right hand of the throne of God.*

Remember, friends, when we see the word "therefore" in the Bible, we need to ask, "What's that therefore, there for?" The writer is saying, "Now that you have all of that information about the people of faith in chapter 11, live this way..." It is a call to make application in light of the information that you now possess.

These in chapter 11 make up the great cloud of witnesses. They have run their race, even though they hadn't yet received their reward. Now, it's time for us to run our race. They looked ahead to the One who was coming and to the city whose architect and builder is the Lord. They endured suffering, hardship, and persecution. They were challenged, tested, and it took all that they had. And they were faithful.

On the other side of the cross, we are to look to Jesus, the author and perfecter of our faith. We are to see what he endured and know it was worth it, because something better was coming. It was so much better that, "...for the joy that was set before him endured the cross..."

What is this joy? I believe it was the eternal throne, seated at the right hand of the Father. It is here in Hebrews 12 that it is noted that Jesus "...is seated at the right hand of the throne of God." This is the fourth time in Hebrews this is stated. This enthronement signifies victory. One writer says, "Jesus assumed that triumphant position at the right hand of the throne of God (cf. 1:3; 8:1; 10:12) which presages His and the believers' final victory (cf. 1:13–14)."[71]

It is this coming victory that we long for and press on toward. As a result, we are to throw off all sin that entangles us and run with perseverance and endurance the race marked out for us.

In 1968, the Summer Olympics were held in Mexico City. During the marathon, John Stephen Akhwari of Tanzania fell badly, dislocating his knee and injuring his shoulder. Most athletes would have quit. He was hurt, in last place, and limping badly. In fact, doctors urged him to stop running. But Akhwari pressed on. Hours after the winner had crossed the finish line and the stadium lights were being shut off, he hobbled into the arena. Only a few thousand spectators remained, but they watched in awe as he painfully limped the last lap.

When asked later why he didn't just quit, he said something unforgettable:

"My country did not send me 5,000 miles to start the race. They sent me 5,000 miles to finish it."[72]

That's the picture of Hebrews 12:1. Runners in the ancient world would literally strip off their outer garments so nothing would weigh them down. No distractions. No extra weight. No unnecessary baggage. Just the race.

In our walk with Christ, faith calls us to lay aside anything that slows us down — habits, hidden sins, fears, doubts, even good things that have become distractions. Why should we do this? Because we are called to finish. Like Akhwari, we don't run just to start the race of faith — we run to finish it faithfully, with endurance, with our eyes fixed on Jesus.

What weight are you carrying today that is slowing down your race of faith? Is there a habit, fear, or hidden sin that clings too closely? Lay it down at the feet of Jesus. Write it out, confess it, and ask God for the strength to run unhindered. Remember, Jesus is better!

Prayer

Lord, show me the weights I am carrying that slow me down in following You. Give me the courage to lay aside sin, distractions, and anything that pulls my eyes off You. Strengthen me to run with endurance the race You have set before me, until the day I see You face to face. Amen.

Endnotes

1. Bible Sense Lexicon, Logos Bible Software, title (deed).

2. Ibid., convicting evidence.

3. Bible Sense Lexicon, Logos Bible Software, end (point of time).

4. Ibid, firstborn.

5. Neal, D. A. (2016). Enoch. In J. D. Barry, D. Bomar, D. R. Brown, R. Klippenstein, D. Mangum, C. Sinclair Wolcott, L. Wentz, E. Ritzema, & W. Widder (Eds.), The Lexham Bible Dictionary. Lexham Press.

6. Logos Bible Software, Logos Bible Sense Lexicon, "walk."

7. Roger Steer, George Müller: Delighted in God (Wheaton, IL: Harold Shaw Publishers, 1997), 45–50.

8. Christian History Institute, "Prayer Like the Falling of Many Waters," Christian History, accessed August 2025, https://christianhistoryinstitute.org/magazine/article/ch153-korea. The article recounts how, in the aftermath of the Korean War, elderly women—often widowed or raising grandchildren—gathered at dawn to weep and pray faithfully for revival, today known as part of the rise of South Korea into a mission-sending nation.

9. Warren Wiersbe, Weirsbe's Expository Outlines, 1992, Logos Bible Study Software, accessed July 17, 2025.

10. Billy Graham, Just As I Am: The Autobiography of Billy Graham (San Francisco: HarperCollins, 1997), 20.

11. Graham, Just As I Am, 20.

12. Ibid.

13. Wiersbe, W. W. (1992). Wiersbe's expository outlines on the New Testament (p. 707). Victor Books.

14. Brunson, Andrew. God's Hostage: A True Story of Persecution, Imprisonment, and Perseverance. Baker Books, 2019.

15. Cathy, S. Truett. Eat Mor Chikin: Inspire More People. Looking Glass Books, 2002.

16. Fyre Festival," Wikipedia, last modified August 25, 2025, https:// en.wikipedia.org/wiki/Fyre_Festival.

17. N.J. Opperwall, The International Standard Bible Encyclopedia, Logos Bible Study Software, Accessed July 18, 2025.

18. Barry, J. D., Mangum, D., Brown, D. R., Heiser, M. S., Custis, M., Ritzema, E., Whitehead, M. M., Grigoni, M. R., & Bomar, D. (2012, 2016). Faithlife Study Bible (Heb 11:17). Lexham Press.

19. Peterson, D. G. (1994). Hebrews. In D. A. Carson, R. T. France, J. A. Motyer, & G. J. Wenham (Eds.), New Bible commentary: 21st century edition (4th ed., p. 1345). Inter-Varsity Press.

20. Wiersbe, W. W. (1996). The Bible exposition commentary (Vol. 2, p. 319). Victor Books.

21. Elliot, Elisabeth. Through Gates of Splendor. Tyndale House Publishers, 1981.

22. Peterson, D. G. (1994). Hebrews. In D. A. Carson, R. T. France, J. A. Motyer, & G. J. Wenham (Eds.), New Bible commentary: 21st century edition (4th ed., pp. 1347–1348). Inter-Varsity Press.

23. Achtemeier, P. J., Harper & Row and Society of Biblical Literature. (1985). In Harper's Bible dictionary (1st ed., p. 751). Harper & Row.

24. Enduring Word Bible Commentary Hebrews Chapter 11

25. Wiersbe, W. W. (1996). The Bible exposition commentary (Vol. 2, p. 319). Victor Books.

26. Glenn W. Wagner, "Grandpa Taught Me How to Fish," Michigan Conference of the United Methodist Church, May 6, 2019, https:// michiganumc.org.

27. Genesis 48:19-21.

28. "The Root of Beautiful Patience," Desiring God, accessed August 2025, https://www.desiringgod.org/interviews/the-root-of-beautiful-patience.

29. Ibid.

30. Ibid.

31. Harriet Tubman Resources, National Park Service, accessed August 2025, https://www.nps.gov.

32. Harriet Tubman Biography, National Women's History Museum, accessed August 2025, https://www.womenshistory.org.

33. Harriet Tubman: Visions of Freedom, PBS documentary and companion website, accessed August 2025, https://www.pbs.org.

34. Harriet Tubman: Quotes and Legacy, Library of Congress, accessed August 2025, https://www.loc.gov.

35. Public Domain: First published 1878.

36. Baker Encyclopedia of the Bible, pp 952–955.

37. Ibid.

38. John Newton, An Authentic Narrative of Some Remarkable and Interesting Particulars in the Life of John Newton (1764); Bruce Hindmarsh, John Newton and the English Evangelical Tradition (Oxford University Press, 1996).

39. Craig S. Keener, Miracles: The Credibility of the New Testament Accounts (Baker Academic, 2011), pp. 502–506.

40. Kenyon, Excavations at Jericho, 1957; Wood, Did the Israelites Conquer Jericho?, Biblical Archaeology Review, 1990.

41. Ibid.

42. Chrissy Outlaw, testimony in I Was Wrong: Why the World's Most Notorious Atheist Called It Quits by Lee Strobel (interview reference).

43. Amy Grant et al., Faithful (Colorado Springs, CO: David C Cook, 2021), 21.

44. John F. MacArthur Jr., Twelve Extraordinary Women: How God Shaped Women of the Bible and What He Wants to Do with You (Nashville, TN: Nelson Books, 2005), 62.

45. Adolph L. Harstad, Joshua, Concordia Commentary (Saint Louis, MO: Concordia Pub. House, 2004), 142.

46. O. S. Hawkins, The Bible Code: Finding Jesus in Every Book in the Bible (Nashville, TN: Thomas Nelson, 2020).

47. Spurgeon, The Spurgeon Study Bible: Notes (Nashville, TN: Holman Bible Publishers, 2017), 274.

48. Hawkins.

49. Harstad, 142.

50. Summary of Rahab's Scarlet Cord, Logos Bible Software, accessed, August 18, 2025.

51. John G. Nicolay and John Hay, Abraham Lincoln: A History, Vol. 6 (New York: Century Co., 1890), p. 183.

52. Allen C. Guelzo, Lincoln's Emancipation Proclamation: The End of Slavery in America (Simon & Schuster, 2004).

53. Booton Herndon, The Unlikeliest Hero: The Story of Desmond T. Doss, Conscientious Objector Who Won His Nation's Highest Military Honor (Pacific Press Publishing, 1967); Congressional Medal of Honor Society, "Desmond T. Doss," cmohs.org.

54. U.S. Olympic & Paralympic Museum, "Glenn Cunningham: Miracle Mile Runner" (usopm.org).

55. Robert Falcon Scott, Scott's Last Expedition: The Journals (London: Smith, Elder & Co., 1913).

56. Roland Huntford, The Last Place on Earth: Scott and Amundsen's Race to the South Pole (Modern Library, 1999).

57. Helen Keller, The Story of My Life (New York: Doubleday, 1903).

58. Dorothy Herrmann, Helen Keller: A Life (Knopf, 1998).

59. 2 Maccabees 6:18–31; 2 Maccabees 7:1–42 (NRSV Apocrypha).

60. 2 Maccabees 7:1–42, NRSV Apocrypha.

61. F. F. Bruce, The Epistle to the Hebrews, The New International Commentary on the New Testament (Grand Rapids: Eerdmans, 1990), 321–323; William L. Lane, Hebrews 9–13, Word Biblical Commentary, Vol. 47B (Dallas: Word, 1991), 361–363.

62. Hastings, J., Selbie, J. A., Lambert, J. C., & Mathews, S. (1909). In Dictionary of the Bible (p. 791). Charles Scribner's Sons.

63. Hastings, J., Selbie, J. A., Lambert, J. C., & Mathews, S. (1909). In Dictionary of the Bible (p. 792). Charles Scribner's Sons.

64. Email sent to me, August 26, 2025.

65. United States Commission on International Religious Freedom (USCIRF), 2025 Annual Report on Eritrea, April 2025, https://www.uscirf.gov/sites/default/files/2025-04/Eritrea%202025%20USCIRF%20Annual%20Report.pdf.

66. "Martyrs of Abitinae." Wikipedia. Last modified July 20, 2025. https://en.wikipedia.org/wiki/Martyrs_of_Abitinae.

67. Blandina: A Sister in Christ and a Spiritual Mother, The Gospel Coalition | Canada, accessed August 2025, https://ca.thegospelcoalition.org.

68. F. F. Bruce (The Epistle to the Hebrews, NICNT, 1990).

69. "Day of the Christian Martyr: Christians Persecuted in Mosul Iraq (2014)," Voice of the Martyrs, accessed August 2025, https://www.persecution.com.

70. "Ten Years after IS Captured Mosul, Believers Still Feel Unable to Return," Open Doors International, accessed August 2025, https://www.opendoors.org.

71. Hodges, Z. C. (1985). Hebrews. In J. F. Walvoord & R. B. Zuck (Eds.), The Bible Knowledge Commentary: An Exposition of the Scriptures (Vol. 2, p. 810). Victor Books.

72. "John Stephen Akhwari." Wikipedia. Last modified March 25, 2024. https://en.wikipedia.org/wiki/John_Stephen_Akhwari.

Bibliography

1. Achtemeier, P. J., Harper & Row and Society of Biblical Literature. *Harper's Bible Dictionary.* 1st ed. San Francisco: Harper & Row, 1985.

2. Barry, J. D., Mangum, D., Brown, D. R., Heiser, M. S., Custis, M., Ritzema, E., Whitehead, M. M., Grigoni, M. R., and Bomar, D., eds. *Faithlife Study Bible.* Bellingham, WA: Lexham Press, 2012, 2016.

3. Bruce, F. F. *The Epistle to the Hebrews.* The New International Commentary on the New Testament. Grand Rapids: Eerdmans, 1990.

4. Brunson, Andrew. *God's Hostage: A True Story of Persecution, Imprisonment, and Perseverance.* Grand Rapids: Baker Books, 2019.

5. Cathy, S. Truett. *Eat Mor Chikin: Inspire More People.* Atlanta: Looking Glass Books, 2002.

6. Elliot, Elisabeth. *Through Gates of Splendor.* Carol Stream, IL: Tyndale House Publishers, 1981.

7. Graham, Billy. *Just As I Am: The Autobiography of Billy Graham.* San Francisco: HarperCollins, 1997.

8. Guelzo, Allen C. *Lincoln's Emancipation Proclamation: The End of Slavery in America.* New York: Simon & Schuster, 2004.

9. Harstad, Adolph L. *Joshua.* Concordia Commentary. Saint Louis: Concordia Publishing House, 2004.

10. Hastings, J., Selbie, J. A., Lambert, J. C., and Mathews, S., eds. *Dictionary of the Bible.* New York: Charles Scribner's Sons, 1909.

11. Herrmann, Dorothy. *Helen Keller: A Life.* New York: Knopf, 1998.

12. Hodges, Z. C. "Hebrews." In *The Bible Knowledge Commentary: An Exposition of the Scriptures,* edited by John F. Walvoord and Roy B. Zuck, Vol. 2, 785–833. Wheaton, IL: Victor Books, 1985.

13. Huntford, Roland. *The Last Place on Earth: Scott and Amundsen's Race to the South Pole.* New York: Modern Library, 1999.

14. Keener, Craig S. *Miracles: The Credibility of the New Testament Accounts.* Vol. 2. Grand Rapids: Baker Academic, 2011.

15. Keller, Helen. *The Story of My Life.* New York: Doubleday, 1903.

16. Lane, William L. *Hebrews 9–13.* Word Biblical Commentary, Vol. 47B. Dallas: Word, 1991.

17. MacArthur, John F., Jr. *Twelve Extraordinary Women: How God Shaped Women of the Bible and What He Wants to Do with You.* Nashville: Nelson Books, 2005.

18. Nicolay, John G., and John Hay. *Abraham Lincoln: A History.* Vol. 6. New York: Century Co., 1890.

19. Opperwall, N. J. "International Standard Bible Encyclopedia." In *Logos Bible Study Software.* Bellingham, WA: Faithlife.

20. Peterson, D. G. "Hebrews." In *New Bible Commentary: 21st Century Edition,* edited by D. A. Carson, R. T. France, J. A. Motyer, and G. J. Wenham, 4th ed., 1315–1350. Downers Grove, IL: Inter-Varsity Press, 1994.

21. Scott, Robert Falcon. *Scott's Last Expedition: The Journals.* London: Smith, Elder & Co., 1913.

22. Spurgeon, Charles H. *The Spurgeon Study Bible: Notes.* Nashville: Holman Bible Publishers, 2017.

23. Steer, Roger. *George Müller: Delighted in God.* Wheaton, IL: Harold Shaw Publishers, 1997.

24. Strobel, Lee. *I Was Wrong: Why the World's Most Notorious Atheist Called It Quits.* Interview reference, includes Chrissy Outlaw's testimony.

25. Wagner, Glenn W. "Grandpa taught me how to fish." *The Michigan Conference of the United Methodist Church.* May 6, 2019.

26. Warfield, Benjamin B. Various writings on providence, quoted in secondary sources. Princeton Theological Seminary, 19th–20th c.

27. Wiersbe, Warren W. *The Bible Exposition Commentary.* Vol. 2. Wheaton, IL: Victor Books, 1996.

28. *Wiersbe's Expository Outlines on the New Testament.* Wheaton, IL: Victor Books, 1992.

Online Sources

1. Baker Encyclopedia of the Bible. Grand Rapids: Baker Publishing.

2. Christian History Institute. "Prayer Like the Falling of Many Waters." *Christian History*. Accessed August 2025. https://christianhistoryinstitute.org/magazine/article/ch153-korea.

3. Desiring God. "The Root of Beautiful Patience." www.desiringgod.org/interviews/the-root-of-beautiful-patience.

4. Enduring Word Bible Commentary. Hebrews Chapter 11. www.enduringword.com.

5. National Park Service (nps.gov).

6. National Women's History Museum (womenshistory.org).

7. PBS. *Harriet Tubman: Visions of Freedom.* Documentary and companion website.

8. Logos Bible Study Software.

9. Library of Congress. "Harriet Tubman Quotes and Legacy."

10. Open Doors. "Ten Years After IS Captured Mosul, Believers Still Feel Unable to Return." www.opendoors.org.

11. The Gospel Coalition | Canada. "Blandina: A Sister in Christ and a Spiritual Mother."

12. USCIRF. *2025 Annual Report: Eritrea.* www.uscirf.gov/sites/default/files/2025-04/Eritrea%202025%20USCIRF%20Annual%20Report.pdf.

13. Voice of the Martyrs. "Day of the Christian Martyr: Christians Persecuted in Mosul Iraq (2014)."

14. U.S. Olympic & Paralympic Museum. "Glenn Cunningham: Miracle Mile Runner." www.usopm.org.

15. Congressional Medal of Honor Society. "Desmond T. Doss." www.cmohs.org.

www.ingramcontent.com/pod-product-compliance
Lightning Source LLC
LaVergne TN
LVHW052023080426
835513LV00018B/2128